fl 1-15

D0959446

A Blueprint for Discipleship

Wesley's General Rules as a Guide
for Christian Living

Kevin M. Watson

DISCIPLESHIP RESOURCES

P O BOX 340003 • NASHVILLE, TN 37203-0003
www.discipleshipresources.org

Cover design by Shawn Lancaster
Interior design by PerfecType, Nashville, TN

ISBN 978-0-88177-556-3

Library of Congress Control Number: 2008943679

Scripture taken from the HOLY BIBLE, TODAY'S NEW INTERNATIONAL VER-
SION®. TNIV®. Copyright© 2001, 2005 by International Bible Society. Used
by permission of Zondervan. All rights reserved.

A BLUEPRINT FOR DISCIPLESHIP: Wesley's General Rules as a Guide for
Christian Living. Copyright © 2009 Discipleship Resources. All rights reserved.
No part of this book may be reproduced in any form whatsoever, print or
electronic, without written permission.

For information regarding rights and permissions, contact Discipleship
Resources, PO Box 340003, Nashville TN 37203-0003; fax 615-340-1789.

Discipleship Resources® and design logos are trademarks owned by GBOD®,
Nashville, Tennessee. All rights reserved.

Contents

Acknowledgments

The idea for this book came as the result of a keynote address I was invited to give on Wesleyan Spirituality at McFarlin United Methodist Church in Norman, Oklahoma, in September 2007. I am grateful for the invitation and for the thoughtful questions and encouragement I received from those who attended. This was a homecoming of sorts for me, as it was at McFarlin that I first began to feel a calling to ministry, and it was there that I received support and nurture as I began to gain confidence in my calling. Phil Fenn, Dick House, and Scott Meier all have taken an active interest in supporting me over the years.

I would like to offer thanks to the many people who graciously provided feedback on this book at various stages. A group of clergy in the Enid District of the Oklahoma Conference kindly volunteered to read an early draft, providing helpful feedback. Gail Edmison, Jim Edmison, Robert Foos, Dane Lemmons, Steve Littrell, and Carolyn Murrow were a part of this group. Andrew Conard, Gary Holdeman, Matt Judkins, and Scott Meier also read drafts. I would be remiss not to thank the church that I was serving in while I wrote most of this book, Lamont United Methodist Church in Lamont, Oklahoma; thank you for your support and encouragement over our three years together. George Donigian and Doug Hagler at Discipleship Resources made themselves available to my frequent questions and showed me what grace looks like in the world of publishing. Finally, this book, for many reasons, would not have been possible without the love, support, and encouragement provided by my wife Melissa, to whom this book is dedicated.

Introduction

Much has been made recently about the perception that there is a growing gap between the way Christians ought to live and the way that they actually live. A recent book, *UnChristian: What a New Generation Really Thinks about Christianity . . . and Why It Matters,*[1] discusses research which suggests that people outside of the church often see Christians as people who have many "unchristian" attitudes. Christians are seen as hypocritical, only concerned with getting people "saved," homophobic, sheltered, too political, and judgmental. In another book, *The Scandal of the Evangelical Conscience*, Ron Sider argues, "scandalous behavior is rapidly destroying American Christianity."[2] Indeed, many people are noticing that Christians are not living up to some of the most basic teachings of their own faith.

This gap between the gospel's expectations for believers and the day-to-day actions of professing Christians is all the more important when seen in relation to the reality that American culture is changing. Perhaps it has already changed, and we are just now starting to notice.

Author and pastor Dan Kimball has noted recently that in past generations almost every person in America was likely to be at least a nominal Christian. However, according to Kimball, "Today things are quite different. We are living in a pluralistic culture. . . . [but] most Christian leaders aren't aware of this change going on."[3] We used to be able to assume that people would be introduced favorably to the church simply by growing up somewhere in the United States. Today, however, we cannot assume that people are going to become Christians simply by growing up in America. In fact, the problem may be much deeper than we first thought. People who are not Christian often don't see going to church as merely unnatural; even more alarmingly, they often see church as boring, useless, and irrelevant.

Mainline denominations, such as the United Methodist Church, should be particularly concerned about these trends. United Methodism has seen numerical decline for more than four decades. Nearly everyone in the denomination recognizes that we cannot afford to continue doing things the way we have been doing them for the last forty years.

No matter what our denominational background, it seems that most Christians in America are struggling to practice their faiths. At the same time, we also appear to live in a culture where people are increasingly turned off by a church that does not practice what it preaches. If this is true, we who are in the church have a problem. Yet, I have been frustrated with how many books seem to raise these issues without offering much in the way of answers or providing a way forward. It seems obvious that we have a problem. But what is the solution? Perhaps a story will illustrate why it is not enough merely to point out that there is a problem.

Once upon a time, I was curled up on the sofa, absorbed in a great book. Gradually, a slight smell of smoke began to intrude upon my reading. At first, I didn't really notice. The thought entered my mind, "The neighbors must be cooking out." The smell of smoke continued to get stronger and stronger. I started feeling somewhat hot, but I just told myself that it is July and it is ninety-five degrees outside. I convinced myself that I was hot because it was hot outside. But then I began to realize that the living room was getting brighter and brighter. This was odd because it was about nine in the evening. Finally, I put the book down and looked up. Immediately, I realized that something was very wrong. There was smoke pouring into the room from the hallway, and I could see flames coming out of the bedroom. I got up in a daze, stumbled outside, and watched the house burn to the ground.

Fortunately, this did not actually happen. I hope, though, that if I ever smelled smoke in my house, I would be a bit more proactive. I know if I realized that my house was on fire, I would not be content simply to walk outside and pull up a chair and watch the fireworks. Ultimately, coming up with the proper diagnosis, if I did nothing about it, would still mean that my house would burn down. In order to save my home, I would need to take immediate action. Calling the fire department would be a great place to start!

Similarly, as United Methodists look at the spiritual landscape, our avoidance of the reality that most of our churches are in decline is done at our own peril. Yet, if we only proclaim the demise of the UMC with an increasingly shrill voice, the predictable result will be despair. It is not enough to diagnose the problem without a solution.

One of the most pressing and immediate challenges facing the church in the twenty-first century is living as if the message of Jesus Christ were true. Methodists and other Christian traditions seem to have two basic options in the immediate future. We can desperately hold on and try not to lose too many members too quickly. That is, we can try not to die. But surely merely surviving is not God's deepest desire for the church. The much preferable option is that we choose to live, not by our own power, but by stubbornly deciding to depend on God's grace, by breathing deeply of God's Spirit, and by heading out into the world and allowing our lives to give witness to who Christ is and what he has done for us. Either way, we have a decision to make. And we need to remember that the world is watching, as is our Lord.

Like the church, individual Christians who face reality also seem to have two basic options. As individuals, we can give up hope and give in to despair. Methodists, for example, can decide that Methodism is clearly in its twilight years, and we can decide to do what we can to make our own death more comfortable. Again, I cannot see this as God's desire for Methodism.

Alternatively, we can repent of our collective and individual sins and turn our lives over to God. We can stop allowing the magnitude of the problem to paralyze us and start looking for positive and creative ways to respond to the problem. I have not met very many people who have become involved in the life of a congregation because the people already in the church needed them so desperately. I have met far more people who entered into the life of a congregation because they had a desperate need that only Jesus could meet. A good place for us to start, then, would be to stop focusing on how to get what we want from other people and instead to focus on how we can share with others the good news that Christ offers us.

Given the context in which Methodism finds itself, this book seeks to do two things. Broadly, it argues for the need for a more robust understanding of discipleship. In order to appeal to a larger audience, the church has recently made the mistake, in my view, of watering down the expectations that come with being a disciple of Jesus Christ. Too often a desire to be relevant to a larger audience has resulted in the broader culture transforming the church more than the church fulfilling its calling to be salt and light to the world around it.[4] In the Gospel of John, Jesus says, "If you hold to my teaching, you are really my disciples."[5] In other words, this book will argue for the need to make a deep commitment to becoming a disciple, one who lives the kind of life that Jesus taught his followers to live.

More particularly, this book seeks to make a contribution to the efforts of the particular community of faith that I have been set apart to serve within, the United Methodist Church, and its efforts to make disciples of Jesus Christ. A major conviction of this book is that the Wesleyan heritage of the United Methodist Church (and other

Wesleyan traditions) has a specific approach to making disciples that has proven successful in the past and has an important contribution to make to our efforts to make disciples in the present and future. Therefore, while I certainly hope and pray that this book benefits people from many different parts of the Body of Christ, I have chosen primarily to focus on the "Methodist" approach to discipleship. This book will seek to address the following questions: Does being a part of the Wesleyan tradition make any difference as we face the challenge of living out our faith in Jesus Christ? Does our heritage offer any specific guidance for us as we look to the future and seek renewal?

This book is the result of my conviction that the answer to both of these questions is *yes*. I believe the world is desperate for Christians who are not just hearers of the Word, but for Christians who are doers of the Word. Many Christians sense that there is more to the Christian life than what they have experienced so far. Many people are ready for a deeper and more meaningful relationship with God, but they aren't quite sure where to start or how to find it.

Happily, Methodists are direct descendants of one of the most gifted organizers and strategic leaders in the history of the church, John Wesley. Wesley instituted a method in early Methodism that was designed to make sure Christianity was not just a set of beliefs, but that it actually became a way of life. Wesley outlined the Methodist approach to making disciples in an essay called the General Rules, and this essay is receiving increasing attention. While many in the church today might dismiss the idea of submitting to rules, or a rule of life, Wesley and the early Methodists found that covenanting together to do three things provided a framework for enabling them to move forward in their faith and grow closer to God. The General Rules were: 1) do no harm; 2) do all the good that you can; and 3) attend on the ordinances of God (or, practice the spiritual disciplines).

In the pages to come, we will examine the importance of grace for empowering and enabling growth in the Christian life. We will look closely at each of the General Rules, keeping an eye on their relevance for twenty-first-century Christians and the ways in which the General Rules help us to find and maintain balance in our lives as Christians. (Appendix A includes the complete text of the General Rules.) Finally, we will examine the other crucial aspect of the Methodist method, "watching over one another in love," through a small-group accountability structure. (To this end, Appendix B provides a guide for small groups.) The hope is that the reader will discover, or rediscover, Methodism's potential for helping those who want to follow Jesus become, by God's grace, deeply committed Christians who have life-changing, contagious faith. This book will not only argue that it is possible to become a fully devoted follower of Jesus Christ, but it will also provide practical, straightforward suggestions for how to allow God to enter more and more deeply into your life until you find that it is difficult to tell where you end and God begins.

Endnotes

1. David Kinnaman, and Gabe Lyons, *UnChristian: What a New Generation Really Thinks About Christianity . . . and Why It Matters* (Grand Rapids: Baker, 2007).
2. Ronald J. Sider, *The Scandal of the Evangelical Conscience: Why Are Christians Living Just Like the Rest of the World?* (Grand Rapids: Baker, 2005).
3. Dan Kimball, *They Like Jesus but Not the Church* (Grand Rapids: Zondervan, 2007), 168-170.
4. See Matthew 5:13-16.
5. John 8:31 *(TNIV)*.

1

Grace: The Foundation for Wesleyan Faith

What Is Grace?

What would you do if a stranger asked you to define "grace"? Would you run away? Would you mumble, "I dunno." Would you spray mace in this face? (Not a very grace-ful reaction!) Would you confidently give your textbook definition? Or would you tell a story about how you have experienced God's grace in your own life?

When I was in seminary, I went very sleepily to my evangelism class early one Friday morning. I saw the three-hour class as the last thing standing between me and the weekend. The professor's indication, however, that we were going to go out into Washington, D.C., to ask random people three questions about their spiritual lives woke me up faster than any amount of coffee!

I have to be honest with you. I don't even remember what the first two questions were that we were supposed to ask. But I clearly remember the third question: "What is grace?" This question sticks in my mind because I remember being terrified that someone would respond, "I don't know. What is grace?" I didn't know what I would say if the question were turned back on me. As our class members came back to report on our experiences, we learned that most people did not have a good idea of what grace is. People had opinions about Christians, Christianity, and Jesus, but they did not quite know what to say about grace. What would you say if someone asked you, "What is grace?"

This is a crucial question because grace is the foundation of the Christian life. According to scripture, grace plays a primary role in our salvation: "For it is by grace you have been saved, through faith—and this is not from yourselves, it is the gift of God—not by works, so that no one can boast."[1] Grace is the source of our salvation. Grace is the reason that we can have hope when we begin to realize the extent of the distance that we have put between ourselves and God. According to the letter to the Ephesians, we are saved by grace through faith. Thus, Wesley and many other influential Christian leaders insist that even our ability to have faith is grace-empowered. It is not an exaggeration to say that grace empowers the Christian life every single step of the way.

All this is to say that before we can talk about how to practice our faith, we first have to talk about God's grace.

While it is tempting to move immediately to the specifics of what we need to do in order to be faithful Christians, we need to take the time to make sure we properly orient ourselves before we start. We need to make sure we recognize the central role that grace plays in our journeys as followers of Jesus Christ. Before we can talk about the specifics of the method that Wesley and his followers used for helping Christians become disciples of Jesus Christ, we first have to lay the foundation that the method is built on—the grace of God. It is grace that causes us to realize that we need God, that brings us to faith, and that brings us as new Christians to the place where we can ask, "What's next?"

God Does for Us What We Cannot Do for Ourselves

So, what *is* grace? Scripture encourages us to "know the grace of our Lord Jesus Christ, that though he was rich, yet for your sake he became poor, so that you through his poverty might become rich."[2] This passage seems to indicate that God's grace reaches down to lift us up. Grace is God's action on our behalf to work to save us when we cannot save ourselves. God is complete and sufficient, and, apart from God's grace, we are neither complete nor sufficient. Grace is God's love that seeks to restore us when we cannot restore ourselves and when we do not deserve to be restored.

Frankly, grace is a far more radical concept than most of us are comfortable with. Many theologians who have gone before us have wrestled with the implications of this concept. Even Paul, the writer of a significant portion of the New Testament, struggled with grace. In 2 Corinthians, Paul writes about having a "thorn in the flesh" that he asked God to take away from him. Paul recounts that God's response was not simply to remove the thorn, but to remind Paul to rely on grace: "My grace is sufficient for you, my power is made perfect in weakness."[3] What a good place to start! Grace is God's power made perfect in weakness.

Grace is God's doing for us what we cannot do for ourselves. We see grace in Jesus' determination to seek and save the lost during his ministry on earth. We also see grace in Jesus' determination to seek and save the lost in the days immediately following the crucifixion. And we experience grace in our own lives because of Jesus' determination, despite all that we have done to get in the way, to continue to seek and save the lost today.

Given the strong emphasis in the New Testament on this theme, it is not surprising that one of the major focus of John Wesley's preaching was that salvation was by grace through faith. In his sermon "Salvation by Faith," Wesley preached, "Grace is the source, faith the condition, of salvation."[4] In another sermon, he wrote, "Ye are thus saved, not by any power, wisdom, or strength which is in you or in any other creature, but merely through the grace or power of the Holy Ghost, which worketh all in all."[5] Wesley was thus in full agreement with Ephesians 2:8-9, which he quoted frequently in his sermons, "It is by grace you have been saved . . . not by works."

Wesley further preached that, "the grace or love of God . . . is free in all, and free for all."[6] Grace is free in all because "it does not depend on any power or merit in man."[7] And it is free for all because Wesley found in scripture that, "God so loved the world that he gave his one and only Son, that whoever believes in him shall not perish but have eternal life."[8]

Some of us may have become so familiar with these ideas that we recognize them without actually letting them penetrate deeply into our souls. The Christian faith teaches that God wants to save us when we are at our worst. God loves us still. God is not ignorant of our sin; God sees it more devastatingly than we do. But God loves each one of us and sees someone whom God wants to redeem and make new. Think back to the words that Paul heard from Jesus: "My grace is sufficient for you, for my power is made perfect in weakness."

It is essential to keep grace at the center of the conversation when we talk about growth in the Christian life. We must remember that grace is the major power source that gives energy to all of our efforts to grow in our faith.

Wesley's Heartwarming Experience with Grace

For John Wesley, talking about grace was more than theological sport or describing abstract ideas. Wesley experienced the importance of grace in a powerful way in his own life. He discovered the truth that salvation is by grace and not by works by trying to earn his own salvation as determinedly as he possibly could. He tried to live on his own power for the first thirty-five years of his life. In fact, even after deciding to become a minister in the Anglican church in 1725, Wesley still sought to earn God's favor by his own determined efforts. During his time at Oxford University, Wesley and others formed a group known as the "Holy Club." They became well known for their disciplined and rigorous way of living together. They held each other accountable for reading scripture and praying. They even began to visit prisoners and feed and clothe the poor in the city of Oxford. Yet, Wesley would come to realize that something was missing.

In 1735, Wesley decided to travel to Georgia. He went to America hoping to preach the gospel to those who had not been exposed to it. However, after many years of astonishing dedication and discipline, Wesley was powerfully confronted with the reality that he was missing all that Christianity had to offer. As Wesley traveled by boat to Georgia, fierce storms that threatened to sink the ship interrupted the journey several times. Wesley was terrified. He realized that he was afraid to die and that he did not know what would happen to him if he did. After ten years of working as hard as he could to be a good Christian, he still did not know if God loved him. He did not know if he was good enough. The problem was, if his salvation was conditioned on being good enough, there was always doubt, because he could always find some part of his life that would not hold up under the light of God's judgment.

Wesley recorded part of his experience during one point when the storm was particularly severe and he noticed a stark contrast between the behavior of the English Christians and that of a group of German Christians, both of whom were on the ship. After the storm, he wrote in his journal:

> In the midst of the psalm wherewith their service began the sea broke over, split the mainsail in pieces, covered the ship, and poured in between the decks, as if the great deep had already swallowed us up. A terrible screaming began among the English. The Germans calmly sung on. I asked one of them afterwards, "Was you not afraid?" He answered, "I thank God, no." I asked, "But were your women and children afraid?" He replied mildly, "No; our women and children are not afraid to die."[9]

This experience left Wesley feeling very uneasy and concerned about his relationship with God. He questioned whether he was really a Christian! Isn't it amazing that this man, whose later work was used by God to spark a movement that caused so many people to enter into a relationship with Jesus Christ, doubted whether he was really a Christian at all? The peace demonstrated by the German Christians made such an impact on Wesley that he began to teach himself German so that he could converse with them and learn more from them. He then began to ask them about the source of their confidence in the face of the real possibility of losing their lives.

Wesley recorded one of these conversations in his journal, a conversation which, initially, actually increased his fear that something was missing in his life. He was talking with one of the leaders of the German Christians, August Spangenberg:

> I . . . asked his advice with regard to my own conduct. He said, "My brother, I must first ask you one or two questions. Have you the witness within yourself? Does the Spirit of God bear witness with your spirit that you are a child of God?" I was surprised, and knew not what to answer. He observed it, and asked, "Do you know Jesus Christ?" I paused, and said, "I know he is the Savior of the world." "True,' replied he, 'but do you know he has saved you?" I answered, "I hope he has died to save me." He only added, "Do you know yourself?" I said, "I do." But I fear they were vain words.[10]

Ultimately, Wesley came to realize that his faith was incomplete. He believed that Jesus was the Savior of the world, but he did not know God's love for him personally. He believed that Jesus had died for the sins of the world, but he did not know that Jesus had died for him. He eventually left America in spiritual turmoil, desperately seeking answers. You can sense his anguish in a journal entry written nearly two years after his experiences in 1736:

I went to America to convert the Indians; but Oh! who shall convert me? Who, what is he that will deliver me from this evil heart of unbelief? I have a fair summer religion. I can talk well; nay, and believe myself, while no danger is near: but let death look me in the face, and my spirit is troubled. Nor can I say, "To die is gain!"[11]

Can you sense Wesley's frustration and confusion? Wesley's spiritual journey helps us realize that grace was not simply something that he wrote about in his sermons. Grace was something Wesley came to realize he desperately needed. He realized that he could not save himself. He tried harder than most people ever do, and still he discovered that he could not earn his way to heaven. It is astonishing to think of this man—who had spent countless hours reading the Bible, praying, and even feeding the hungry, clothing the naked, and visiting those who were in prison—as having such overwhelming doubts about whether he was loved by God.

Many Methodists have heard about Wesley's famous experience at Aldersgate Street on May 24, 1738. This was the moment when Wesley was finally given assurance that Christ had saved him, by God's grace. Wesley carefully recorded in his journal this life-changing encounter with God's grace. In this famous account of his experience, Wesley describes the forgiveness of his sins and the long-awaited assurance of his salvation for which he had yearned:

In the evening I went very unwillingly to a society in Aldersgate Street, where one was reading Luther's Preface to the Epistle to the Romans. About a quarter before nine, while he was describing the change which God works in the heart through faith in Christ, I felt my heart strangely warmed. I felt I did trust in Christ, Christ alone for my salvation, and an assurance was given me that he had taken away *my* sins, even *mine*, and saved *me* from the law of sin and death.[12]

This journal entry makes sense only when we understand it in light all that had happened before that evening. Wesley had dedicated himself to a disciplined practice of his faith for more than twelve years, and he had been wrestling with the recognition of his own lack of faith for more than two years! In remembering this, we can begin to glimpse the joy and relief that Wesley must have felt.

After wanting truly to trust Christ for years, that night Wesley discovered that he did trust in Christ for his salvation. He experienced an assurance that his sins had been forgiven and that he had been saved from the consequences of those sins. Paul's words in Romans 8:16 became real in Wesley's own life: "The Spirit himself testifies with our spirit that we are God's children."

Grace at the Beginning, Middle, and End

We would do a great disservice to Wesley's understanding of discipleship, therefore, if we neglected to insist that grace be kept in its proper place at the beginning, middle, and end of all that is said about the Christian life. A key realization is that we can only begin the journey of becoming a disciple of Jesus Christ by God's grace. Grace empowers our conversion and fuels growth in our relationship with God.

It took Wesley more than a decade figure this out. But on May 24, 1738, he experienced the truth that no matter how hard he worked, if he attempted to be holy by his own power, it would never be enough. As disciplined as Wesley's spiritual practice had been, he realized that there was still something missing. He read scripture constantly, prayed frequently, and he fasted once, and often twice, a week. It is not as if he didn't try hard enough. In fact, Wesley tried just about as hard as anyone can. And his efforts simply confirm that no one is saved by his own effort. He realized that he could only be made right with God through faith in Jesus Christ and the gracious forgiveness that comes through him.

For Wesley, then, grace permeates every part of the Christian life. We come to an awareness of our need for God by grace. We are forgiven and made new by grace. And we are enabled to participate in our salvation by grace. It is important to get this clear up front, because as we think about how to live out the Christian life, we need to remember that grace empowers us every step of the way. God's grace is given to us freely and without charge. This grace is the fuel that gives us the power to grow in our lives with God. Thus, any discussion of "working out your salvation"[13] from a Wesleyan perspective must begin and end with God's amazing grace.

We certainly must insist that salvation is a result of the free and undeserved gift of God. This means that when we proclaim the gospel (whether from a pulpit or in a conversation over a cup of coffee), we should talk about God in a way that appropriately expresses the good news that "Christ Jesus came into the world to save sinners."[14] Far too often, we consciously or unconsciously attach conditions to God's free offer of salvation. We need to be very careful not to add obstacles to someone's coming to Jesus that Christ himself has not placed there.

Having stressed the importance of grace as strongly as possible, I also want to acknowledge that Wesley was determined to avoid presuming upon grace. A major part of Wesley's genius was that he was able to explain justification in a way that actually enhances the role and importance of our own participation. One of the major tensions that Christians have struggled with over the years is finding the balance between grace and works, or license and legalism. Various groups of Christians have tended to overemphasize one at the expense of the other. Yet the New Testament clearly emphasizes the importance of both grace and works.

The emphasis on grace and works is particularly seen in Ephesians 2. When people emphasize grace at the expense of works, they cite this chapter and stop with verse 9. However, if our perspective were to expand by just one more verse, we would see the importance of both grace and works more clearly:

> For it is by grace you have been saved, through faith—and this
> is not from yourselves, it is the gift of God—not by works, so that

no one can boast. *For we are God's handiwork, created in Christ Jesus to do good works, which God prepared in advance for us to do.*

Salvation, according to Ephesians, is certainly received by the free and unmerited gift of God's grace. Unfortunately, some Christians have closed their Bibles immediately after reading verse 9 and ignored verse 10. As a result, a rationalization can develop for not dealing with one's continual sin that goes something like, "There is nothing I can do to earn God's favor. Works are the things that people do who have not learned to rely upon God's grace."

While we insist that salvation is God's free offer to us, we also need to remember that there is a tenth verse in the second chapter of Ephesians. This verse could be seen as the answer to the questions: What are we saved for? What does God purpose in our salvation? The answer: "We are God's handiwork, created in Christ Jesus to do good works, which God prepared in advance for us to do." Ultimately, a faithful reading of Ephesians 2 would strongly encourage Christians to practice their faith.

In the next chapter, I will say more about the role that grace plays in enabling us to participate in our salvation. For now, it is important for you to ask yourself a few questions: Have you had an encounter with the amazing grace of God? Is there someone like August Spangenberg in your life to ask you if the Spirit of God bears witness with your spirit that you are a child of God? Maybe you have been working as hard as you can to live faithfully like a Christian for many years, maybe even for as long as you can remember. For some of us, it is very difficult to see our need for salvation. It is difficult to renounce our own goodness. But grace is good news, not bad! The good news is that God loves you. You don't have to earn God's favor; in fact, you cannot.

Charles Wesley wrote a hymn that is still in the United Methodist Hymnal titled "Come, O Thou Traveler Unknown." The hymn is based on the story of Jacob wrestling all night with God, in Genesis 32:22-32. At the end of the hymn, Charles' lyrics lead us to recognize that the One we have been wrestling with is God, whose very nature is love:

'Tis Love! 'tis Love! Thou diedst for me,
I hear thy whisper in my heart.
The morning breaks, the shadows flee,
pure, Universal Love thou art.
To me, to all, thy mercies move;
thy nature and thy name is Love.
To me, to all, thy mercies move;
thy nature and thy name is Love.[15]

Questions for Discussion

1. What is grace? How would you answer this question if someone were to ask you?

2. What is your reaction to the summary in this chapter of Wesley's spiritual journey as it is summarized?

3. When have you experienced the power of God's grace in your life? How are you experiencing God's grace in your life today?

4. How would you answer August Spangenberg's questions if he were to ask you, instead of Wesley: "Does the Spirit of God bear witness with your spirit, that you are a child of God?" "Do you know Jesus Christ?" "Do you know he has saved you?"

5. Are you willing to renounce your own goodness in order to find the love and grace of God? What would this require of you?

6. Reread Ephesians 2:8-10. How does verse 10 change your understanding of this passage?

Endnotes

1. Ephesians 2:8-9 (*TNIV*).
2. 2 Corinthians 8:9 (*TNIV*).
3. 2 Corinthians 12:9 (*TNIV*).
4. *The Works of John Wesley*, Vols. 1-4, *The Sermons*, ed. Albert C. Outler, "Salvation by Faith" (Nashville: Abingdon Press, 1984), 1:118.
5. *Sermons* "The Means of Grace," 1:383.
6. *Sermons* "Free Grace," 3:544.
7. *Sermons* "Free Grace," 3:545.
8. John 3:16 (*TNIV*).
9. *The Works of John Wesley*, Vols. 18-24, *Journals and Diaries*, eds. W. Reginald Ward and Richard P. Heitzenrater (Nashville: Abingdon Press, 1993), 18:143.
10. *Journals and Diaries*, 18:145-146.
11. *Journals and Diaries*, 18:211.
12. *Journals and Diaries*, 18:249-250.
13. Philippians. 2:12 (*TNIV*).
14. 1 Timothy. 1:15 (*TNIV*).
15. Charles Wesley, *The United Methodist Hymnal* "Come, O Thou Traveler Unknown"(Nashville: United Methodist Publishing House, 2000), 386.

2

Participation in Our Growth as Disciples: The Goal of Grace

A few years ago, a man and a woman met, dated for a while, and fell in love. It wasn't long before the man found himself getting down on one knee and asking the woman if she would marry him. With tears in her eyes she said, "Yes." And then it seemed as if the couple lost control of things. The wedding planning took months and months. Everything had to be perfect. There was so much work to do. Sometimes it felt as if their wedding day would never arrive because they were so excited to be husband and wife. On other days, it felt as if it were coming too fast because there was still so much that had to be accomplished. Eventually, though, everything got done, and the wedding went wonderfully.

Before they knew it, they were on their honeymoon, on a beautiful beach. They slept in late and were finally feeling well rested. The sun was shining, and they were watching the waves lap onto the beach, one after another. They didn't have a care in the world because they had made it. They were married! And the best part was that they both knew that the hardest part was behind them. All they had to do now was to live out the rest of their lives together joyfully and without a care in the world.

As husband and wife were lying side by side in their lounge chairs, he closed his eyes, felt the warmth of the sun's rays on his eyelids, and smiled. He knew that their life together was going to be everything he had ever wanted from a marriage. He was excited finally to get to eat some decent home-cooked food. He was glad that he would not have to worry about the dirty clothes that kept piling up in his room. He was so at peace that he began to think about bringing children into the world with this amazing woman. He knew that he wanted to have two kids, like his own family. Life was good.

Meanwhile, she was also smiling, gazing through her sunglasses out toward where the ocean blended into the horizon. She had never been happier. And though she wanted simply to rest in this moment, she couldn't help dreaming about their future lives together. She was looking forward to doing everything together: cooking, cleaning, redecorating every room of the house (because she was moving into his place and it needed some work). And like him, she could see their lives unfolding into the future. She could clearly see their beautiful family, all five kids that she had always wanted to have, just like her family. Life was good.

These two people sound as if they may be in for a few surprises! It may seem ridiculous to think that two people could get married and never have talked about things as significant as who was going to cook or how many children they wanted to have. But if you have been married, or have known someone closely who is married, you have probably witnessed the look of utter shock and confusion on someone's face when they suddenly realize, "The life I have always assumed we would have is not the same life that my spouse always assumed we would have."

Just the Beginning

Sometimes we make the mistake of assuming that the beginning of something is the end. The couple in our story thought they had arrived in the promised land. But anyone who has been married, even if only for one year, knows that they are only getting started. Certainly, there will be many great and joy-filled days. But there will also be many days that are hard.

We don't just confuse beginnings with endings when thinking about marriage. We seem to have a tendency to approach major decisions with a sense of finality: What do I want to be when I grow up? Do I want to try to have children? Should I move? Should I change careers? In all of these things, we are making very important decisions, and those decisions can bring a sense of relief or release at having found "the answer" to what we were looking for. Sometimes we forget that though making a decision marks the end of the decision-making process, the decision itself does not become reality until our lives reflect it.

For instance, think about the honeymoon period in a marriage, the time when the spouse seemingly can do no wrong. Eventually, that period ends. Nobody has to tell the couple when it is over; they just know! For some people, the honeymoon period lasts only as long as the honeymoon itself. For others, the honeymoon ends while they are still on the honeymoon! For others, it is much later. But it is around this time that one begins to have the uncomfortable feeling that being married is going to take more work than getting married did. Getting married is the easy part. It is fun. People give presents, and they stand while the couple walks down the aisle. But in a successful marriage, both people eventually understand that being married takes work, and then they commit to growing together in love for the rest of their lives.

Unfortunately, Christians also seem to make the mistake of confusing the beginning of something with its end. There is an abbreviated form of Christianity that has become popular in recent years. It can be expressed in a simple statement: "I got saved." When I hear someone say this, I cringe.

The main reason this statement is inadequate is that it suggests that all that really matters in people's spiritual lives is one significant experience. They need to "get saved." Nothing they do before or after that moment is very important. When the church adopts this approach to Christianity, there is a lot of effort put into simply asking people if they have received Jesus Christ as their Lord and Savior. If the answer is "Yes," then we can check that person off our list. If they say, "No," then all of our effort is focused on trying to getting those persons to come to a place where they will pray one prayer, often called the sinner's prayer.

What Are the Odds?

Once, while living in the dorms at the University of Oklahoma, I was doing some homework when there was a knock on the door. I opened the door to see the faces of two guys I had never seen before in my life. They were both holding clipboards, and they looked very serious. My first thought was: what have I done wrong?

One of them mumbled something about where they were from and asked if he could ask me a few questions. I said, "Sure," though I have to admit I wanted to say, "No." I don't remember anything more that he said, except for one question. He showed me a chart that had a "0" on the far left side and a "100" on the far right side. He asked me, "If you were to die today, what percent chance do you think you would have of going to heaven, from zero percent to one hundred percent?" I said, "One hundred percent." This was my honest reaction, based on my relationship with God and the assurance that I had that I had become one of God's children.[1] But I also assumed that was the answer they were looking for. If I had said anything less than one hundred percent, they would ask me if I wanted to know how I could be one hundred percent sure that I would go to heaven when I died. The odd thing was that although I gave the answer he was looking for, he seemed surprised and perhaps a bit disappointed at my response.

My visitors were trying to figure out if I was really a Christian, or if I was just hoping to "sneak in" to heaven when I died. If I had said I wasn't sure that I was going to heaven, then they would have explained that Jesus died so that I could be forgiven and that all I had to do in order to be saved was to ask Jesus into my life by praying. So, in the language that we were speaking, I had just told them that I was a born-again follower of Jesus Christ, and the visitor seemed disappointed! I hoped he would rejoice that I was his brother in Christ. Instead, he mumbled, "Umm, Ok. Thanks." And then he and his friend left.

I may be painting a bit of a one-sided picture here. I would be the first to say that the United Methodist Church and most mainline Protestant denominations have a lot of room to grow when it comes to being willing to share the gospel with others. Passages of scripture such as 1 Peter 3:15 challenge me: "Always be prepared to give an answer to everyone who asks you to give the reason for the hope that you have." We need to be willing to share the gospel and to invite people to make a decision to invite Jesus into their lives. As stated previously, we need to insist that salvation is always by grace.

My point is this: There is more!

Looking back, I wish the guys who had come to my dorm room had followed up their question by asking, "Is there anything we can do to help you live out the faith in Jesus that you have found?" Even better would have been, "That is awesome! Have you found a church here in town that you are comfortable going to? If not, we are a part of a church that we really like, and we would love for you to come with us to worship sometime." But from their perspective, I was already saved and that was all that really mattered, so they moved on to the next room.

Praying the sinner's prayer is not the end goal of the Christian life. Praying one prayer, or having one experience of God's grace, is not the fullness of what God hopes for us. Please don't misunderstand me: having an initial experience of God's grace by faith is absolutely essential, but it does not represent the entirety of the Christian life.

When we talk about "getting saved," we sound a lot like the naive couple on their honeymoon who think that they have experienced the fullness of marriage. They will soon realize that getting married is just the beginning of marriage, not the end. Similarly, receiving forgiveness of our sins and being born again do make us Christians: "Once we were not a people, but now you are the people of God."[2] There is a real change, but it is just the beginning of an entirely new way of life.

Saved for Something

If we are born again when we put our faith in Jesus, for what are we born again? I think this is one of the key areas where Methodists and other Wesleyans have such an important spiritual contribution to make to the church universal. We come from a tradition that affirms the need for people to come to faith in Jesus Christ and to be born again. We also come from a faith tradition that says we are born into a new way of life. We are born again so that we can live for God. It is a sadly abridged version of the gospel that considers the new birth the extent of salvation. The scriptures proclaim that Jesus came so that we might have life "and have it abundantly."[3] Wesley affirmed that Jesus died to save us from hell and to save us for something!

One of the distinctive marks of Wesleyan theology, therefore, is the way in which John Wesley balances grace and works. For Wesley, grace is essential, but our participation with God's grace is also critical. As theologian Randy Maddox has stated it, Wesley preserves "the vital tension between two truths: . . . without God's grace, we *cannot* be saved; while without our (grace-empowered, but uncoerced) participation, God's grace *will not* save."[4] Another way of looking at this is to understand that before we come to faith in Christ and receive forgiveness of our past sins, we cannot even be considered to be responsible for our actions because we are in chains to sin. God's grace makes us responsible once again. This same grace also makes us able to respond to God's grace and begins to work out our salvation.

Grace is a crucial foundation because it enables us to participate in our own growth in holiness. For Wesley, the Christian life is not over once we enter into a relationship with Jesus Christ. Instead, following Christ enables us to participate with God's gracious renewal of our lives in the image of God. This is the way that we participate in the Holy Spirit's work of sanctifying us, or making us holy. Wesley discussed this in a sermon he preached on Matthew 5:17-20 (in the Sermon on the Mount where Jesus says that he has not come to abolish the Law or the Prophets). Listen to Wesley's comparison of the righteousness of a Pharisee versus the righteousness of a Christian:

> The righteousness of a Christian exceeds all this righteousness of a scribe or Pharisee by fulfilling the spirit as well as the letter of the law, by inward as well as outward obedience. In this, in the spirituality of it, it admits of no comparison. This is the point which our Lord has so largely proved in the whole tenor of this discourse. Their righteousness was external only; Christian righteousness is in the inner man. The Pharisee "cleansed the outside of the cup and the platter"; the Christian is clean within. The Pharisee laboured to present God with a good life; the Christian with a holy heart. The one shook off the leaves, perhaps the fruits of sin; the other "lays the axe to the root", as not being content with the outward form of godliness, how exact soever it be, unless the life, the spirit, the power of God unto salvation, be felt in the inmost soul.[5]

Perhaps this description of the goal of the Christian life could be just as well summarized with the words that Jesus spoke when a Pharisee asked him what the greatest commandment was in the law. "Jesus replied: 'Love the Lord your God with all your heart and with all your soul and with all your mind.' This is the first and greatest commandment. And the second is like it: 'Love your neighbor as yourself.' All the law and the prophets hang on these two commandments."[6] The goal of Christianity, according to Wesley, is not merely to do certain outward things, although this is certainly the most visible aspect of Wesleyan spirituality. The ultimate goal is to be completely renewed in the image of God, to be made perfect in love. Wesley defined this as fulfilling Jesus' double commandment to love God (with all your heart and with all your soul and with all your mind) and to love your neighbor as yourself.

We all have some experience acting toward someone in a way that is very different from how we feel toward them on the inside. You can be civil to someone when you interact in a public atmosphere, while harboring resentment or bitterness toward him or her in your heart. This is the kind of hypocritical spirituality that Wesley condemned and insisted that we avoid. He wanted Christians to become people who are not only outwardly nice, but who also actually love God and all people with whom they come into contact.

This distinction gets at the basic difference between deeply committed Christians and nominal Christians. We tend to put deeply committed Christians up on a pedestal in a way that makes it obvious that "normal" people could never live like that. We think of Mother Teresa and say, "I could never live in the slums of Calcutta and take care of the sick. I have my own family to take care of and look after." On many different levels, we compare our lives negatively to those who have done incredible things for the kingdom. Instead of putting others up on a pedestal and saying to ourselves, "I could never do that," perhaps we would do better to look around and ask, "What can I do?" The difference between deeply committed Christians and everybody else may be simpler than we think. Deeply committed Christians are people who give their lives completely to God. They are people who exercise their wills in cooperation with God's grace to follow Jesus in everything that they do. Sometimes this leads people to Calcutta. At other times, it leads people to stay right where they are, loving the people whom God has already placed before them and spending unseen hours on their knees in prayer.

Exploring All of God's House

Few adults watch a seven-year-old play the piano and think, "I wish I could play the piano that well." On the other hand, we may marvel at the talent and skill possessed by a concert pianist. However, concert pianists must start somewhere. Their first recital may not have turned any heads. It may have even made some people want to plug their ears! Similarly, our efforts to live faithfully may not turn heads or cause people to sing our praises. Instead, our faith tells us that even the smallest action done with a desire to please God does not go unnoticed by our Father who is in heaven.

The goal of grace, then, is not just to save us from ourselves; it is to enable us to enter into a deeper and deeper relationship with God so that we are able to love God and our neighbor increasingly. Wesley described the different ways that grace works in our lives by using the illustration of God's house. Wesley argued that God's prevenient grace (the grace that goes before us) keeps us from moving farther away from God. Prevenient grace wakes us up and causes us to realize that we need to be saved. It brings us to repentance. Wesley compared grace working in this way to the front porch of God's house, meaning that God's prevenient grace brings us to repentance and (figuratively speaking) onto the front porch of God's house.

Once we find ourselves on the porch of God's house, God's grace works to get us in the front door. Through justifying grace, we are enabled to have faith in Jesus Christ and to find forgiveness of our sins. At the same moment that we are forgiven, we are born again. Our old way of life dies, and we are raised in Christ into a new life. Wesley believed that scripture teaches that we can know that we have entered into God's house by the witness of the Spirit where "the Spirit himself testifies with our spirit that we are God's children."[7] We really can be one hundred percent sure of our salvation!

Wesley's analogy also helps us to see how much more there is to the Christian life than being forgiven of our sins and being born again.

Can you imagine how amazing it would be if God literally had a house? If I were invited into God's house, to explore every part of the house, I cannot imagine that I would be content to stand in the entryway for the rest of my life. Yet isn't that what so many of us do? We think, "Well, I have made it inside. I'm set! Now I can go back to the things that were important to me before." Too many people, when they articulate their version of the gospel, leave a person standing just inside the door. Too many of us, if we are honest, have been standing on the porch or just inside the door of God's house for years.

Wesley reminds us that once we are in the house, God wants us to live in it. God doesn't want us just to look around as if we are in a museum or on a tour, admiring the beauty and splendor as a spectator. No! God's invitation is not only to come and see where God lives. God is actually inviting us to move in! We are invited to live with God. God's sanctifying grace works to transform us from people who lived by ourselves in our own shacks into people who live in communion with God and our neighbors under one roof.

Too often, we want to place our little toe inside God's house, while the rest of us continues to live in the filth and squalor of our former homes. The questions with which Wesley wants us to wrestle are: Why are we content to settle for less than what God wants for our lives? Why are we content to begin the process of salvation but not to finish it? In 1 Corinthians Paul asks, "Why start running a race if you have no intention of finishing it?" He wrote to the Corinthians:

> Do you not know that in a race all the runners run, but only one gets the prize? Run in such a way as to get the prize. Everyone who competes in the games goes into strict training. They do it to get a crown that will not last; but we do it to get a crown that will last forever. Therefore I do not run like someone running aimlessly; I do not fight like a boxer beating the air. No, I strike a blow to my body and make it my slave so that after I have preached to others, I myself will not be disqualified for the prize.[8]

The scriptures teach us that Jesus wants to transform us, that when we are born again, we are not at the end of our spiritual journeys, but we have just begun. When we give our lives to Christ, we are starting a new way of living because Jesus wants us to follow him with our very lives.

Wesley was so convinced of this concept of a full life in Christ that he worked diligently to do all that he could to encourage those who became Christians under his care to move into God's house. He did all that he could to encourage Methodists to continue growing in holiness. Wesley was so convinced that God wants us to be deeply committed to our faith that he created a method to help it to happen.

Wesley knew that people did not automatically move from a confession of faith into a completely transformed life. In fact, if anything, when people were left on their own, the tendency was that they gradually moved back to their old ways of living. Wesley, therefore, created a structure that brought people together in order to "watch over one another in love." This structure of accountability happened in a large worship gathering and then through smaller levels of support. He also created a specific guide for new Christians that communicated how they could grow in their relationships with God. These General Rules consisted of three simple guidelines that Wesley believed would help people grow in their relationships with God.

This communal and individual structure for how to practice one's faith was the Methodist blueprint for how new Christians could become disciples. Wesley was convinced that this method would lead people into a deeper and deeper relationship with God so that they could move their lives into God's house and become more and more like Jesus. In a time when the world seems to be desperate for the witness of Christians who are deeply committed to practicing their faith, this blueprint is as relevant as ever. All people who have taken on the name of Christ by calling themselves Christians would benefit from adhering to a similar blueprint.

1. Have you ever mistaken the beginning of something with the end? Have you ever thought you had arrived at the end of a journey, only to look back in hindsight and realize it was just the beginning? Describe this experience.

2. What is your reaction to the statement that Jesus died not just to save us from hell, but to save us for something? What are some of the things you think Jesus died to save you for?

3. Is God's grace present in your life today? How? Are you growing in your faith, or are you still stuck at the starting line? Why?

4. We will look more specifically at the details of the method of the early Methodists in the next chapter. This method requires a basic commitment not only to profess Christ with our mouths, but also to proclaim faith in Jesus by the way we live our lives. Are you willing to take up your cross and follow Jesus? Prayerfully consider your answer, and then write your response below.

Endnotes

21. See Romans 8:14-16.
22. 1 Peter 2:10 (*TNIV*).
23. John 10:10 (*NRSV*).
24. Randy Maddox, *Responsible Grace* (Nashville: Kingswood, 1994), 19.
25. *Sermons* "Upon our Lord's Sermon on the Mount: Discourse the Fifth," 1:568.
26. Matthew 22:37-40 (*TNIV*).
27. Romans 8:16 (*TNIV*).
28. 1 Corinthians 9:24-27 (*TNIV*).

3

A Method: The Wesleyan Blueprint for Discipleship

John Wesley: Master Organizer

The main reason that we are talking about John Wesley in the twenty-first century is not because of the theology or the ideas that we have discussed in the previous pages. Wesley's genius, and the main reason we remember him, the blueprint he instituted to ensure that Methodists would become faithful followers of Jesus Christ and a holy community. Wesley's goal was not to get as many people as he could to pray a certain prayer. Rather, his goal was to get as many people as he could to trust in Christ, not just for one moment, but for the rest of their lives and with all of their lives.

Wesley was realistic enough to realize that when people came to place their trust in Jesus, they did not magically turn into mature Christians. He recognized that many preachers preached the gospel in a compelling way, leading people to place their trust in Jesus. Yet

Wesley saw the main challenge not as getting people to come to a moment of conversion, but as helping them to live out the decision to give their lives to Christ. Wesley referred to this process of living out one's faith as "sanctification." As a result, one of Wesley's passions was creating a method that brought the Christian faith to life and enabled people to continue to grow in holiness of heart and life. He wanted his followers to discover a relationship with God that supported them throughout their lives, through good times and bad. The Methodist movement sometimes grew so fast that it seemed to be an organizational nightmare. It was the method behind this potential madness that harnessed the outpouring of energy and excitement that so many people were expressing about God.

Have you ever met people who have one amazing idea after another? Their minds are constantly thinking of new things, each idea on a larger scale than the last. They have wonderful ideas, but may not be nearly as good at following through on them. Some people seem to need the change and the excitement that come with new ideas. Wesley understood that for most people, there was an initial rush of excitement and energy that came when experiencing the new life that comes in Christ. But this often represents a limited opportunity, a brief window of time, where people briefly set aside all that they previously knew to be true about the world. During this time, they are willing to rethink everything based on the beauty of the gospel.

Sadly, chances are that if you have encountered someone who has the new energy and enthusiasm that often come from entering into a relationship with Jesus, you have seen someone gradually losing that same energy and zeal. The world and external pressures can wear us down, dulling our passion and enthusiasm for God and the things of God. Wesley saw this happen far too often. As a result, he committed himself to doing whatever he could to create an environment where people could be supported and nurtured so that they could continue to grow in their newfound faith.

Wesley believed in a disciplined religious structure, not because he was a natural bureaucrat and liked to create hoops for people to jump through, but because he saw this structure bear fruit. His experience showed him that when Christians ground their good intentions in a committed way of living, those intentions are much more likely to come to life. On the other hand, when people come to know the love of God shown in Christ Jesus with no support network, no structure, no guidance for what to do next, people often move away from practicing their faith until they eventually don't have anything left that even resemble faith.

Wesley often reflected in his journal on his experiences in ministry. He was not afraid to acknowledge setbacks or failures. For example, in 1763, after witnessing amazing revival through the Methodist movement for twenty-five years, Wesley reflected on Methodism in an area of Wales known as Pembrokeshire. On August 25 he wrote:

> I was more convinced than ever that the preaching like an apostle, without joining together those that are awakened and training them up in the ways of God, is only begetting children for the murderer. How much preaching has there been for these twenty years all over Pembrokeshire! But no regular societies, no discipline, no order or connection. And the consequence is that nine in ten of the once awakened are now faster asleep than ever.[1]

This experience, and others like it, showed Wesley that without discipline, most people eventually drifted back to the ways they had been living. Our experience today shows this to be true, too. It is often easier to coast in our faith in the direction in which our culture leads us. We are inundated with so many messages that draw our attention away from God and encourage us to thirst after things that are of lesser importance than God. If we are not diligent and grounded, we can begin to move away from God without ever realizing what is happening.

Don't Throw Water on the Fire!

Do you remember when you first personally tasted God's love? Do you remember when you first put your trust in Jesus? Were there any desires that came with those feelings? Were there things that you wanted to do that set your heart on fire? Are you doing those things today? Or have you gradually lost the passion that you had when you first experienced God's love?

Many things can influence our lives in ways that distract us from loving and serving God. During my first assignment as a pastor, I remember having a conversation with a much more experienced pastor. I shared what I felt God was teaching me about my strengths and weaknesses as a minister. I was excited and restless because I felt as if I were learning about how I could best use God's gifts to serve the church. He interrupted me and said: "I have heard too many pastors say that they are not gifted for this or gifted for that. That is garbage. You just do it and move on." The message I received from him was that all churches are the same and that my understanding of how God was at work in my life was irrelevant. I have heard other pastors say that they were specifically told by "veteran" pastors that they should expect to get crusty and disillusioned with the ministry.

These are lies! If people have ever told you that you should expect to lose your passion for serving God and for becoming a fully committed follower of Jesus Christ, what they are saying may be more a reflection of the lack of passion they are feeling in their own relationship with God than anything else. God does not call us all to serve in the same way. The Creator lovingly and intentionally created each one of us to be gifts to the world in certain specific and unique ways.

We are all different. That isn't a mistake. Sometimes, Christians act as if a lack of passion, contentment with the status quo, and apathy are marks of Christian maturity. That belief is closer to blasphemy than the truth. Jesus expects his followers to grow in their understandings of what it means to be his follower, and he expects his followers to grow in their abilities to practice what he teaches. This does not look like complacency or spiritual stagnation; it looks like growth and maturity in Jesus Christ.

Wesley refused to accept spiritual apathy from the people who joined his movement. He insisted that people who joined Methodism commit to a way of living that would help them move forward and become more and more Christ-like. He asked people about their spiritual lives, how God was moving, and how they were responding to the promptings of the Holy Spirit. The early Methodists expected their relationship with Jesus Christ to transform them.

Do you expect your relationship with Jesus Christ to change you? When is the last time someone asked you how God is working in your life, or how you are doing spiritually? One of the reasons United Methodists and many other mainline denominations are struggling may be because we have stopped expecting that being a Christian will change our lives. Author Dallas Willard has lamented, "for at least several decades the churches of the Western world have not made discipleship a condition of being a Christian . . . . So far as the visible Christian institutions of our day are concerned, *discipleship clearly is optional.*"[2] Somehow, Christians have come to believe that it is possible to be a follower of Jesus without actually following the teachings or way of living that Jesus taught. No wonder people who are not Christians think we are hypocrites!

We have tamed Christianity so that it no longer challenges us. We have muted Christianity so that those around us can no longer hear any evidence of it in the music of our lives. But we can do better. We must do better. Jesus laid down his life for us so that we might live, and so that we might be a sign to the world of the power of the coming kingdom of God. When we sit in church on Christmas Eve and feel the peace and excitement of Jesus coming into the world because of God's love for us, and when we enter the sanctuary on Easter morning and hear the good news that Christ is risen, how can we walk out of the building and go back to life as usual?

Isn't there something more? Are you ready for something more?

Wesley looked at the church of his day, the Church of England,

and the lack of commitment from most people who called themselves Christians deeply troubled him. He even preached a sermon at Oxford University where he accused all the religious people there of being "almost" and not "altogether" Christians. Wesley preached, "Are not many of you conscious that you never came thus far? That you have not been even 'almost a Christian'?"[3] Wesley was angry that people were missing God's best for them. He was angry that people who had taken on the name of Christ were making Christianity look so irrelevant and unappealing.

After Wesley experienced the power of God's grace at Aldersgate Street, he began to preach with a power that he had not had before. People began to resonate with the message he preached and the urgency with which he preached it. But he didn't stop there. He also began to create a structure that would help keep us awake to the reality that God wants every part of our being. God wants to transform us until every chain of sin, even the very root of original sin, is pulled up from their lives. Wesley was so methodical in this task in his own life, even before Aldersgate, that people began mockingly to call him and the others in his group, "Methodists."

Methodical Methodists

What was the method behind Methodism? The method consisted of two key parts. The first part was a structure that organized people into smaller and smaller groups so that they could connect to each other and give an account of how they were growing in their faith; the second part was a guide for how individuals should practice their faith in Christ. This guide was summarized in an essay Wesley wrote called "The Nature, Design, and General Rule of Our United Societies," which is commonly referred to as "The General Rules." This essay is still printed in *The Book of Discipline of the United Methodist Church*. "The General Rules" outlines how Christians can, by God's grace, become deeply committed followers of Jesus Christ. These three rules are: 1) Do no harm; 2) Do all the good that you can; and 3) Attend upon the ordinances of God. In the next three chapters, we will consider specifically what each one of these meant to the early Methodists and what they might mean for us today.

The first part of the Wesleyan method helped connect individual people to each other so that they would not be isolated individuals trying to go it alone. This method of organization consisted of three layers of fellowship: the society meeting, the class meeting, and the band meeting. The society meeting was the largest level of organization, where the people gathered to worship God. The society meeting was very similar to today's congregational worship. At the society meeting, people would gather to sing hymns, pray, and hear a sermon that was usually aimed at bringing them to an awareness of their sins and their need for God. It was a wake-up call.

People who experienced an awakening and wanted to know more because of what they experienced at the society meeting were immediately plugged into the next level of organization, the class meeting. The class meeting had seven to twelve people in it. This group met weekly to check in on how each person was doing spiritually. The question, "How is it with your soul?" or "How does your soul prosper?" was asked of each person in the group. This was a way of asking each person, "How are you doing spiritually? How is God working in your life?" This weekly practice helped people form the habit of listening for God in their lives and expecting God to be at work in their lives.

The class meeting was a requirement of early Methodism, and for quite a while, each person had to attend the class meeting in order to get a ticket to go to the society meeting. In other words, if you wanted to attend the fellowship gathering, you had to have a ticket to get in! That is how important Wesley thought the class meeting was. The main advantage of the class meeting was that every single Methodist talked to a trusted, loving group of people under the care of a responsible lay leader about what was happening in his or her life with God. Unfortunately, the class meeting has almost entirely disappeared in United Methodism today.

The final level of organization was the band meeting. In the band meeting, members would confess any sins they had committed and admit to ways they had fallen short, and they would express to one another the forgiveness that Jesus Christ offers them. These groups consisted of about six people. Due to the intense and intimate subject matter—confessing specific sins—the band meetings were divided by gender. And because of their level of intensity, unlike the class meetings, the band meetings were considered optional.

The first part of the Methodist method was the society, class, and band structure that enabled people to get to know each other more intimately and to share their joys and struggles in their faith journeys. The ultimate goal of this method was to create a model that would help Methodists practice their faith and guarantee that they would not only be Christians in name, but also that they would actually become deeply committed followers of Jesus Christ.

The General Rules offer a simple, straightforward path to becoming a deeply committed Christian, the kind of person who will turn on its head the stereotype of Christians who are hypocrites and do not practice what they preach. This kind of person will be someone who commits to avoiding doing anything that will harm him or herself or another person. Committed Christians will do all that they can to help their neighbors grow in faith. They will commit to practicing their faith with disciplined reading of scripture, praying, and joining together with other Christians in the journeys of Christian faith.

The General Rules offer a blueprint that maps out how people who put their faith in Jesus can become disciples of Jesus. This essay by Wesley is one of the key documents that makes Methodism unique and makes it successful in its efforts to make disciples for Jesus Christ.

Planning for Renewal

You may be wondering: why the history lesson? Too often, we hope for good results without ever planning for how those results will actually happen. Wesley did not just hope that the people who responded to his preaching would become mature Christians on their own. Instead, he immediately joined them together so that they could "watch over one another in love." Wesley didn't just hope that good things would happen; he planned for them to happen.

It is important for us to have a basic grasp of Methodist history because it helps us to recognize that when Methodists gave up on the method that I have just described, they gave up on the very process that had been the reason so many people not only had entered into relationships with Jesus Christ, but also had grown into mature Christians. The past is important, not only because it is interesting, but also because it still has an important contribution to make to the church today. The founder of our faith tradition suggested that Methodism would keep its spiritual vigor and vitality only as long as it continued to practice this method. Here are Wesley's own words:

> I am not afraid that the people called Methodists should ever cease to exist either in Europe or America. But I am afraid lest they should only exist as a dead sect, having the form of religion without the power. And this undoubtedly will be the case unless they hold fast both the doctrine, spirit, and discipline with which they first set out.[4]

What conclusions do you think Wesley would come to if he were to survey your church today? Would he find that it has held fast to the "doctrine, spirit, and discipline" that were the keys to Methodism's success? My concern is that many of our churches have abandoned all three of these things almost entirely. My hope is that we will choose to return to these emphases and that in so doing we will find renewal and God's blessing.

We live in a time when many people want to enter into deeper and more meaningful relationships with Jesus Christ. Maybe you are one of those people. Maybe you sense that there is more to being a Christian than what you have experienced, but you aren't sure how to find that deeper meaning. We will look closer at each of the General

Rules in the next three chapters. Ultimately, I think you will find that the method is simple. The question is not, "Can we understand this process?" The question is, "Do we have the discipline to put it into practice?" The way that we answer this question will go a long way toward revealing the depth of our commitment to our faith.

In the Gospel of John, Jesus says, "If you hold to my teaching, you are really my disciples."[5] Are you holding to Jesus' teachings? I hope you will join me as we take a closer look at the plan that those who have gone before us used to help them ensure that they did not merely listen to the Word, but that they actually did what it says. My hope and prayer is that we will become, once again, a community of faith that is known above all else for being doers of the Word.

Questions for Discussion

1. How would you respond to the two questions that were asked earlier in this chapter: Isn't there something more in your spiritual life? Are you ready for something more?

2. Who do you watch over in love? Are you involved in any kind of small-group accountability? If not, would you be interested in being involved in a small group? Why?

3. How do you think Wesley would evaluate contemporary Methodism's faithfulness in holding fast to the "doctrines, spirit, and discipline" that were key to early Methodism's success?

4. What is keeping you from holding fast to Jesus' teachings?

Endnotes

1. *Journals and Diaries*, 21:424.
2. Dallas Willard, *The Great Omission: Reclaiming Jesus' Essential Teachings on Discipleship* (San Francisco: Harper, 2006), 4.
3. *Sermons* "The Almost Christian," 1:140.
4. *The Works of John Wesley*, Vol. 9. *The Methodist Societies: History, Nature, and Design*, ed. Rupert E. Davies, "Thoughts Upon Methodism" (Nashville: Abingdon Press, 1989), 527.
5. John 8:31 (*TNIV*).

4

The First Rule: Do No Harm

The Kids Who Became Parents

Have you ever noticed that kids don't always respond positively to rules and regulations? In fact, they seem to have this precious inner need to test rules and boundaries that are placed before them. To this day, my mom relates the story that every time she told me not to touch something I had to touch it one more time before I stopped.

Parents often encounter a dilemma when faced with children who are testing the boundaries placed on their environment. Either they can bear down, enforce the rules, and hope that they eventually will take hold, or they can give in to their children and try to put a positive spin on things, saying, "They're just being kids." But have you ever noticed that kids just being kids often come very close to kids being brats? The thing is, every family has rules and regulations. But who is making the rules and enforcing them? Is it the parents or the children?

I was writing this chapter in a coffee shop when I observed a mother with a friend and two children. All four people were sitting at a table. The two women were trying to visit with each other while the two children, a boy and a girl who looked about ten years old, looked bored. The boy began karate chopping a stuffed animal that the girl had. The mom, ignoring her children for as long as her patience allowed her to, eventually told them impatiently to knock it off. Then she started ignoring them again, and they continued doing exactly what they had been doing before. A few minutes later, her patience was exhausted again, and she snapped at them, "Shut up!" I looked up (and so did a few other people in the store), but her kids simply continued doing exactly what they had been doing before as if they had not heard a word. Then a bright idea occurred to her. She gave them some money and sent them off to another store.

I think it is safe to say that I was not the only one who was glad to see them leave. However, I also felt sorry for the poor person working in the store that these two children were going to terrorize, this time with no parents present.

What really hit me, though, was that the kids were the ones in charge. The mother had given up her authority as a parent, and her children had decided that she had to live by their rules. This meant that if she wanted to have a conversation with a friend, she had to try to do it over the sound of her children wrestling and arguing with each other. In what was perhaps their most ingenious move of all, the children had further decreed that if their mother wanted to be in charge temporarily—if she wanted them to behave—she would have to pay for it, literally!

Now, I know it is far easier to sit in a coffee shop in judgment of another parent than it is to be the one to instill the rules in your household. As an outsider, it was obvious that the children, though they were running the show, were not happy. They did not seem to enjoy being brats, but they didn't know how else to behave. They didn't know how to control themselves. They needed an authority figure to teach them. Children may not immediately thank you for having rules and consistently enforcing them, but they do need them.

Our Need for Guidance, Direction, and Discipline

Adults aren't all that different from children; sometimes, they simply have much more expensive toys! We also don't like to be told what to do. The main difference may be that adults can refuse to allow others to tell them what to do. Like children, we also need guidance, direction, and discipline. Within the safety of boundaries, we have the freedom to learn, grow, and discover who we are and who God created us to be.

The General Rules provide precisely the kind of guidance and direction that we need in order to have the freedom to grow in holiness of heart and life. The first General Rule is so obvious that even people who are not Christians would probably agree with it, at least in principle. The challenge of this chapter, then, is to make something very straightforward and simple profound enough to grab your attention. Therefore, for the remainder of this chapter, we will work to allow the obvious to sink in deeply enough to actually begin to transform our lives.

In the General Rules, Wesley begins by discussing the basic premise of Methodism:

> There is one only condition previously required in those who desire admission into these societies, "a desire to flee from the wrath to come, to be saved from their sin."[1]

In other words, it was easy to become a Methodist. All people had to do was want to be saved from their sins. This may be more difficult for Christians today than it used to be. We have become very good at dressing up our sins so that they are socially acceptable and hardly noticeable to those inside the church. This raises an important, though complicated, question: How do you know if someone really desires to "flee from the wrath to come, to be saved from their sins?" In other words, how can you tell the difference between people who give lip service to something without ever letting it affect their lives, and those who is deeply committed to doing whatever it takes to be saved from their sins?

Wesley anticipated this question in the General Rules, writing, "wherever this is really fixed in the soul it will be shown by its fruits."[2] The best way to know if people are serious about their commitment to Jesus is simply to look at the fruits of their lives. This leads to another question: What do the fruits of souls that sincerely desire "to be saved from their sins" look like? This is precisely the question that Wesley answers with the three General Rules. Wesley wanted Christians who are sincerely committed to their faith to allow these rules to mold and shape their lives, by the power of God's grace.

One of the reasons the General Rules have such promise for twenty-first-century Christian practice is that they are ideally suited to moving people from nominal faith to holiness. The General Rules provide a helpful blueprint for a stagnant and spiritually dying church to wake up and realize that there is so much more to being a Christian than we have often settled for. Thus, one of the most important roles that the General Rules can play in the church today is to help nominal Christians begin to wrestle with how to actually practice their faiths. For too long, the United Methodist Church has tolerated and even enabled Christians to be fruitless. Membership in the United Methodist Church has been diluted to the point that it is almost meaningless. The time has come to ask people to practice their faiths, or stop calling themselves Methodists.

Wesley expected his followers to deliberately practice their faith. Wesley wrote, "It is therefore expected of all who continue therein that they should continue to evidence their desire of salvation, *First,* By doing no harm, by avoiding evil in every kind—especially that which is most generally practised."[3]

The first thing Wesley expected those who wanted to stay involved in Methodism to do was to stop doing things that caused harm. In

case we wonder what kind of evil Wesley has in mind that is most generally "practised," he is more than willing to list at least fifteen
examples. Some of them are rather predictable: "taking the name of
God in vain," "profaning the day of the Lord," "drunkenness," and
"fighting." Other items that made the list, however, may be more surprising: "buying or selling uncustomed goods," "giving or taking
things on usury," "singing those songs, or reading those books, which
do not tend to the knowledge or love of God," and my personal
favorite—"the wearing of . . . enormous bonnets."

The Scriptural Foundation of the General Rules

A fair question at this point might be: What is the scriptural basis for
following these rules? After all, didn't I specifically say in the first
chapter that the Christian life is started and sustained by grace? As
Christians, haven't we heard our whole lives that justification is by
grace through faith and not by works? If so, why all this need for rules?
Why begin with such a negative focus, like "do no harm?"

We will address this in more depth in the next chapter, but a quick
glance at the scriptures reveals two things: first, the New Testament is
not an abolition of all rules or guidelines; and second, Jesus is very
comfortable giving instructions on how to live, including what not to
do.

According to Matthew's Gospel, Jesus specifically said, "Do not
think that I have come to abolish the law or the prophets; I have not
come to abolish them but to fulfill them."[4] Perhaps the most obvious
example from scripture of rules that God's people are commanded to
live by is the Ten Commandments.[5] These are, after all, ten rules.
Eight of the Ten Commandments are specific instructions about what
not to do. Our discomfort at being told what not to do may be more
a reflection of the lack of discipline in the twenty-first-century
American Church than anything else. (I am reminded of the children
at the coffee shop who wouldn't listen when they were told that they
couldn't fight while their mother tried to have a conversation with her

friend.) When Jesus was asked which is the greatest commandment in the law, he replied, "Love the Lord your God with all your heart and with all your soul and with all your mind. This is the first and greatest commandment. And the second is like it: Love your neighbor as yourself. All the law and the prophets hang on these two commandments."[6]

One of the main reasons, then, that the General Rules have enormous potential for the church today is that they are basic guidelines that can help us follow the greatest commandment that Jesus gave us.

Stop Moving Away from God

The first General Rule is "do no harm." This is simply saying, if we are going to succeed in loving God and loving our neighbor, we first need to stop doing things that lead us away from God. If we are going to move forward, we have to stop moving backward. Therefore, if we were to update the first General Rule for the twenty-first century, we could say, "Do nothing that causes you to move backwards, or do nothing that leads you away from God."

I had been driving for a few years before I tried to learn how to drive a stick shift. Because I saw myself as an accomplished driver, I was confident that this would be an easy task. I had a good teacher, so I felt as if I picked up the art of driving a standard quickly, so quickly, in fact, that I was almost immediately trusted with the responsibility of driving this car by myself. I have to be honest: I loved it. There was something cool about driving a standard, something that made me feel like a race car driver, even though I was driving a Saturn!

Everything was great until I found myself at a complete stop at a busy intersection almost at the top of a steep hill. I was the first car at the intersection. When the light turned green, I let my foot off the brake, pushed in the clutch, and the car started rolling backwards! I immediately hit the brakes again. This happened several times, and each time the distance between my car and the car behind me shrank.

Finally, I got the car in gear and going forward. I learned an important lesson: when driving a stick shift on a hill, you have to make sure the car isn't going backwards before you can make it go forward!

The first rule, then, reminds us to stop moving away from God. The way individual Christians feel about this rule will likely depend on where in life they find themselves. For some who struggle with addiction, this will be an immediate and obvious challenge that will cause them to look to God's grace for help day-by-day. If we take having a relationship with God seriously, we will take the necessary steps to move toward faithfulness to this rule. For others, this rule may initially seem to be very easy to follow. A brief survey of their lives may cause many people to think that they are doing fine because they never intentionally do anything wrong. These people might be tempted to think that they could check this rule off their lists quickly, considering it accomplished.

Wesley, however, encourages us to take a closer look at our lives. He asks us to take our relationship with God so seriously that we do something that may seem radical in our culture today. He wants us to carefully think about everything that we do and ask whether it encourages us to love God. If something encourages us to love God (or our neighbor), we should do it. If it doesn't, we should not do it. It is that simple.

Now, we could look at this and think, "What a ridiculous standard!" Some might argue that if we were to do this, we would live dull and boring lives. You may not have the courage to say this aloud in church, lest the roof come caving in on your head! Nevertheless, there is a decent chance that some of us are entertaining that thought in the back of our minds as we are reading this.

What if that is a lie? What if it is simply not true that our lives will be more boring if we really live for God first? There often seems to be an unspoken assumption even among many members of the United Methodist Church that it is not possible or desirable to actually take living as Jesus taught us seriously.

Yet, a quick glance at many Americans' lives does not suggest that we are all having a blast and that there is nothing that we can do to improve. Is divorce fun? Is getting a sexually transmitted disease fun? Is alcoholism, drug addiction, or pornography addiction fun? Is wondering if you are going to have enough money to pay the bills fun? Is worrying about whether you are setting an example for your children that you would actually want them to follow fun? The list could go on.

When deciding if you the need to consider whether the things that you do encourage you to love God or distract you from your relationship with God, ask yourself these questions: "Is my life as it is now really what God wants for me? Is this the good life? Or is there something more?"

Perhaps thinking carefully about the ways we spend our time could be a helpful exercise to remind us of what is really of utmost importance. For instance, none of us knows how long we have to live. The only thing we know is that our time on this earth is finite; someday we will run out of time. This should cause us to ask, "Are we spending our time in ways that glorify God or in ways that cause us to forget that there is a God?"

The point is not to be legalistic, but to think about what we are doing and why we are doing it. If we look at it on its face, I think we would all agree that the rule to "do no harm" is an important rule for all Christians to follow. It is undoubtedly a safe bet that all of us would do well to turn away from things that lead us away from God.

Today, we are surrounded by thousands of things that compete for our attention and vie for our loyalties. So many things that want to take up residence in our hearts, and many of these things are not helpful. We need to be aware of the things that can lead us gradually and subtly (or quickly and obviously) to shift our focus away from God.

I am powerfully reminded of this each time I read the story of Peter walking on the water in Matthew's Gospel. The disciples have just been a part of the feeding of the five thousand. Jesus then "made the disciples get into the boat and go on ahead of him to the other side, while he dismissed the crowd. After he had dismissed them, he went up on a mountainside by himself to pray."[9] Jesus was in prayer long enough that when he was done, the boat was "a considerable distance from the land, buffeted by the waves because the wind was against it." Since the disciples couldn't get the boat back to him, he decided to walk out to the boat on the water.

Isn't that amazing! The scriptures testify that Jesus walked on water! And the disciples were certainly surprised. They thought Jesus was a ghost, and they were terrified. Jesus tried to calm their fears by speaking to them: "Take courage! It is I. Don't be afraid."

The part of this story that always captures my imagination is Peter's response. He says, "Lord, if it's you, tell me to come to you on the water." I am not sure that would have been my reaction. I am not sure that my first thought upon seeing someone walking on water would be to ask him to tell me to do it too. But this is exactly what Peter did. And Jesus' response is simply, "Come." So Peter gets out of the boat and walks on the water toward Jesus. Peter is *walking on water* with Jesus. It is hard to believe. And Peter is able to do so for as long as he stays focused on Jesus. As soon as the wind begins to distract Peter (remember it is blowing hard enough that the boat could not come back to the shore), he begins to sink and screams, "Lord, save me!"

This story may be so extraordinary that we fail to notice the obvious, everyday implications that it has for our lives. If we focus on the wind, or anything else, we will lose track of Jesus, and we will begin to sink. We will go backwards. This may be obvious enough that it is merely a simple reminder to stay focused on Jesus. Perhaps that is precisely what the General Rules are at their very best, simple reminders to stay focused on the things that matter most. Those who commit to keeping this rule will find that it is harder to do than it may seem at first glance. Keeping our focus on Jesus takes effort.

An effort to keep Christ at the center of our thoughts for an entire day illustrates the difficulty. Many of us would immediately concede that this would be very difficult, if not impossible. However, the reality that it is difficult to stay focused on Jesus only underscores our need for specific practices that help us to remember whose we are throughout each day. One of the struggles with contemporary Christian practice is that many Christians too easily give up when any spiritual discipline threatens to require too much of them. Wesley recognized the difficulty of keeping our focus on Jesus, so he instituted the General Rules, societies, classes, and bands as guides to help Christians learn to become more focused on the Lord in the midst of the chaos of life.

In Romans, Paul wrote, "Let no debt remain outstanding, except the continuing debt to love one another, for whoever loves others has fulfilled the law. The commandments, 'You shall not commit adultery,' 'You shall not murder,' 'You shall not steal,' 'You shall not covet,' and whatever other command there may be, are summed up in this one command: 'Love your neighbor as yourself.' Love does no harm to its neighbor. Therefore love is the fulfillment of the law."[8]

Love does no harm to its neighbor. If we really believe that there is a God and that this God is known in Jesus Christ, do we really want to argue with the simple guideline of doing no harm? Do we really want to argue about why we should be encouraged to do no harm?

The first General Rule recognizes that we are called as Christians to love God and love our neighbors. But we cannot do either if our lives are moving in negative directions, away from God and God's grace. We would do well to remember Paul's words from Romans, "love does no harm to its neighbor."[9] As Methodists, we are called to take seriously the need to do no harm.

Just like the parent at the beginning of this chapter, someone is in charge of our lives. Who is it? It takes courage to take a careful look and honestly answer this question. As we try to do this, remember that the goal is not for us to be in charge. Rather, the goal is for God to be fully in charge. We are seeking to learn to give more and more of ourselves to God. I will always remember the way one of my seminary professors defined this goal—giving all I know of myself to all I know of God.

Our culture tries to set many other guidelines for our lives, but we best live as God intended if we obey this simple rule: "Do no harm." Do nothing that leads you away from God. In order to move forward, you first have to stop moving backward.

Questions for Discussion

1. What is your reaction to the argument that adults aren't that different from children? Do you agree that adults need guidance, direction, and discipline?

2. This chapter mentions the General Rules as a guide for measuring whether people truly desire "to be saved from their sins." Do you think the General Rules are a helpful guide? What other criteria would you suggest, if any?

3. Do you agree that there is a need for mainstream Christians to move from nominal faith to deeply committed faith? Why? What is the difference?

4. What role do you think rules have to play in the Christian life?

5. The author translates Wesley's wording of the first General Rule as "do nothing which leads you away from God." If you were to put it in your own words, how would you summarize it?

6. What are some things that compete for your allegiance or that can distract you from your focus on God?

Endnotes

1. *Methodist Societies,* "The Nature, Design, and General Rules of the United Societies," 9:70.
2. *Methodist Societies,* "The Nature, Design, and General Rules of the United Societies," 9:70.
3. *Methodist Societies,* "The Nature, Design, and General Rules of the United Societies," 9:70.
4. Matthew 5:17 (*TNIV*).
5. See Exodus 20.
6. Matthew 22:37-40 (*TNIV*).
7. Matthew 14:22-23 (*TNIV*).
8. Romans 13:8-10 (*TNIV*).
9. Romans 13:10 (*TNIV*).

5

The Second Rule: Do All the Good That You Can

Often, Christians are known for what they are against rather than what they are for. In the realm of politics, many conservative Christians are known best for being against abortion, for being against gay marriage, for being against sex before marriage, for being against drinking, or smoking—the list could go on.

Sometimes, when people suggest positive things we can do to make a difference, other people tear down the idea by coming up with countless reasons why it won't work. Perhaps we should covenant together to agree that if someone else is suggesting something positive we can do to make a difference in other people's lives, no one else may say anything negative about the idea unless he or she offers a way to improve it. This would especially help Christians who get stuck looking for the perfect thing to do and end up doing nothing. Ultimately, the only way we can guarantee that we will not make a difference is by doing nothing.

There is an old story that has been fairly worn out, especially by preachers, of a young man who is walking along a beach covered with thousands of starfish. The starfish that had washed up onto the beach would soon die if they were not returned to the ocean. One at a time, the young man bent down, picked up a starfish, and threw it back into the ocean. Someone else came along and observed him and asked, "Why are you doing that? You will never be able to make a dent. There are too many starfish. You can't throw them all back. You will never make a difference." The young man replied by bending down, picking up one starfish, tossing it back into the ocean, and saying: "It made a difference for that one."[1]

As we continue to look at the Wesleyan blueprint for discipleship, perhaps it is helpful to remember the goal of this book, which is to offer a constructive proposal about how to make meaningful progress in the Christian life. Early Methodists used a distinct method to ensure that all of their followers were not Christians in name only, but that they actually became disciples. It may not have been perfect, but it made a difference in many people's lives. We explore the General Rules today with the hope that God will use them to transform our lives.

In the last chapter, we looked at the first General Rule: "Do no harm." We discovered that you cannot go forward until you stop going backward. At times, it may have felt as if the first General Rule was just another list of things that Christians are not supposed to practice. However, this is just the beginning. We have to stop moving backward so that we can begin to move forward. In this chapter, therefore, we will look at the second General Rule: "Do all the good that you can." I will demonstrate in this chapter that being a Christian involves much more than just being against things. Above all else, being a Christian means being dedicated to loving God with all our hearts, souls, minds, and strength, and loving our neighbors as ourselves. This is the essence, according to Jesus, of what it means to be a Christian. Ultimately, this is the foundation Wesley was building on in the General Rules.

In the General Rules, Wesley wrote: "It is expected of all who continue in these societies that they should continue to evidence their desire of salvation, *Secondly,* By doing good, by being in every kind merciful after their power, as they have opportunity doing good of every possible sort and as far as is possible to all men."[2]

Wesley fleshes this out differently than he did in the first General Rule. He lists two specific ways that we are to do good. First, "to their bodies, of the ability which God giveth, by giving food to the hungry, by clothing the naked, by visiting or helping them that are sick, or in prison."[3] Second, we are to do good "to their souls, by instructing, *reproving,* or exhorting all they have any intercourse with; trampling under foot that enthusiastic doctrine of devils, that 'we are not to do good unless *our hearts be free to do it.*'"[4]

By Way of Reminder

Before we go any farther, I want to pause to remind us that the General Rules is a document written as a guide not for preachers, missionaries, or "super Christians," but for every single person who is a Methodist. Wesley took the General Rules so seriously that he would often examine all persons in the different societies (which were the large group meetings) to find out if they were following this way of life. If they consistently failed to live by the General Rules, Wesley would remove them from the membership rolls. Membership in a Methodist society really meant something during John Wesley's life. Methodists were by definition the people who practiced this way of living.

No wonder this was a powerful movement! Can you imagine what a church could do today with one hundred people who are so committed to their relationship with Jesus Christ that they are willing to be accountable to one another for doing all the good that they can? My hope and prayer is that this rule of life can show us the way to become, once again, a people who are known for being deeply committed Christians. As we think about what it means to be a Christian, I believe the General Rules can help us move from a consumer-driven, passive, action-less faith to a Spirit-driven, passionate, active faith. In other words, the General Rules remind us that faith is not merely a set of ideas that Christians assent to. Faith leads to holiness, and holiness is the goal. Faith compels followers of Christ to live in a new way.

Ultimately, we are Christians first and Methodists second. Our heritage as both Christians, generally, and Methodists, specifically, encourages us to be a people who do good by feeding the hungry, clothing the naked, and visiting and helping those who are sick and in prison. Our heritage encourages us to be a people who do good to people's souls "by instructing, *reproving*, or exhorting all they" come into contact with.

Once again, we would do well to remember that Wesley did not make up this standard or pull it out of thin air. Wesley's ideas about what it means to be a Christian came from the Bible, which he invested himself in reading and studying carefully. It is time for Methodists to destroy the idol that many American Christians are hiding behind, the idea that a Christian doesn't need to live as Jesus commanded because salvation is a free gift that comes by grace and not by works. Salvation assuredly is a free gift, but God expects that if we accept this gift, we will allow it to transform our lives. Receiving the gift of salvation by grace, through faith, and not allowing it to transform our lives is like a child receiving the bike he asked Santa for on Christmas and then never riding it! Salvation is a pure gift that we cannot earn through works. However, if we accept the gift of salvation but refuse to allow God's grace to transform our lives, we put our very salvation in danger.

Searching the Scriptures

Let's take this to the scriptures. Much of what Wesley says we should do in the second General Rule comes directly from Jesus' parable about the last judgment in the Gospel of Matthew:

"When the Son of Man comes in his glory, and all the angels with him, he will sit on his glorious throne. All the nations will be gathered before him, and he will separate the people one from another as a shepherd separates the sheep from the goats. He will put the sheep on his right and the goats on his left.

"Then the King will say to those on his right, 'Come, you who are blessed by my Father; take your inheritance, the kingdom prepared for you since the creation of the world. For I was hungry and you gave me something to eat, I was thirsty and you gave me something to drink, I was a stranger and you invited me in, I needed clothes and you clothed me, I was sick and you looked after me, I was in prison and you came to visit me.'

"Then the righteous will answer him, 'Lord, when did we see you hungry and feed you, or thirsty and give you something to drink? When did we see you a stranger and invite you in, or needing clothes and clothe you? When did we see you sick or in prison and go to visit you?'

"The King will reply, 'Truly I tell you, whatever you did for one of the least of these brothers and sisters of mine, you did for me.'"[5]

Scripture clearly teaches that faith leads to action. Faith in Jesus should lead us to do good to others.

Ultimately, Wesley was not trying to do anything new. He was simply preaching Christ. However, my primary interest is not in arguing for the need for Christians to become disciples of John Wesley. Rather, I hope to exhort Christians to become fully devoted disciples of Jesus Christ. The General Rules, in fact, are a model for how to practice Jesus' commandment to love God and neighbor. Consider Mark 12:28-31, for instance:

One of the teachers of the law came and heard them debating. Noticing that Jesus had given them a good answer, he asked him, "Of all the commandments, which is the most important?"

"The most important one," answered Jesus, "is this: 'Hear, O Israel: The Lord our God, the Lord is one. Love the Lord your

God with all your heart and with all your soul and with all your mind and with all your strength." The second is this: "Love your neighbor as yourself." There is no commandment greater than these."

This scripture passage and its parallel in Matthew 22:34-40 are a great frame for the General Rules themselves. Unfortunately, some followers of Christ don't seem to believe that Christians need to do anything to be truly Christian. In fact, some argue that Jesus came to fulfill the law and free us from it. Paul, however, wrote in Romans 3:28-31:

For we maintain that a person is justified by faith apart from observing the law. Is God the God of Jews only? Is he not the God of Gentiles too? Yes, of Gentiles too, since there is only one God, who will justify the circumcised by faith and the uncircumcised through that same faith. Do we, then, nullify the law by this faith? Not at all! Rather, we uphold the law.

Faith does not nullify the law. If we return to Jesus' words again, we find that in the Sermon on the Mount in Matthew 5:17-20, Jesus specifically talked about the relationship between the law and himself:

Do not think that I have come to abolish the law or the prophets; I have not come to abolish them but to fulfill them. Truly I tell you, until heaven and earth disappear, not the smallest letter, not the least stroke of a pen, will by any means disappear from the Law until everything is accomplished. Anyone who sets aside one of the least of these commands and teaches others accordingly will be called least in the kingdom of heaven, but whoever practices and teaches these commands will be called great in the kingdom of heaven. For I tell you that unless your righteousness surpasses that of the Pharisees and the teachers of the law, you will certainly not enter the kingdom of heaven.

And there is also, of course, the very well-known passage from James 2:14-17, which says:

> What good is it, my brothers and sisters, if people claim to have faith but have no deeds? Can such faith save them? Suppose a brother or sister is without clothes and daily food. If one of you says to them, "Go in peace; keep warm and well fed," but does nothing about their physical needs, what good is it? In the same way, faith by itself, if it is not accompanied by action, is dead.

Faith without action is dead. If our faith is only thoughts or beliefs that leave our lives untouched, it is dead. It is worthless. I have to be honest, every time I read this passage in James, it rattles me a little bit. It is easier for me to talk about these things than to live them. Sometimes I have been presented with an opportunities to practice my faith, and I have failed to do so.

Missed Opportunities

When I was in seminary, I remember working on one of my first sermons in a coffee shop in Washington, D.C. That was a dangerous place to work on a sermon because real life was happening all around me, asking me if what I was going to say would make any difference in the lives that people were actually living. As I situated myself and began to study the scripture passage that I was going to preach on, I noticed something that turned my sermon upside down—a homeless man. He was sitting by the fireplace, facing me. I couldn't tell if he was staring at me, but every time I looked in his direction he seemed to be looking right back at me. His presence began to bother me more and more. It was as if God were asking me, "What difference does your faith make for him?"

I began to wrestle with that question. What do I do, what should I do? Part of me wanted to talk to him and buy him some food. But another part of me was terrified. What if I began to love him, really love him? How would I be able to protect myself? On a night when I knew it would be ten degrees below freezing, how would I be able to go back to my dorm room and get into my warm bed when my friend was outside with nothing to protect him from the cold but a threadbare blanket? I wanted to care, but I didn't want to have to care too much. Or maybe I wanted to care for him, but I didn't want to be inconvenienced.

I wonder if those feelings are what is behind many of the objections that we make to helping others. We want to do something to make a difference, but we don't want our lives to be too changed. That night, I am sorry to say that fear won, and I lost an opportunity to love my neighbor as myself. Even years later, that man still periodically examines my faith, seeking to discover if it is living, breathing faith, or if it needs CPR.

John Grisham, the popular novelist, powerfully illustrates the danger that can come from getting too close to a person whose life is very different than your own in *The Street Lawyer*. The main character in the book is a Washington, D.C., lawyer named Michael Brock whose life is changed forever when he is held hostage with several other lawyers in his firm by a homeless man. At some point, Brock realizes that the man is not going to hurt any of them; he is just fed up with how much money they make and their refusal to share any of it with those who are less fortunate.

Just before the homeless man is shot by a SWAT team member, he forces one of the hostages to get each person's income tax return and compare how much money they make to how much money they give. He finds that in the last year the nine lawyers made over three million dollars. Then the homeless man comments:

> You make a lot of money, yet you're too greedy to hand me some change on the sidewalk . . . . All of you. You walk right by me as I sit and beg. You spend more on fancy coffee than I do on meals. Why can't you help the poor, the sick, the homeless? You have so much.[6]

Later, he asks them how much money they have specifically given so that hungry people can eat: "I'm talking about food. Food for hungry people who live here in the same city you live in. Food for little babies. Right here. Right in this city, with all you people making millions, we got little babies starving at night, crying 'cause they're hungry."[7] The answer is none. They have not directly given any money to feed their brothers and sisters in need in the very city they live in.

The result of this experience for the main character is that he leaves the firm where he is about to become a partner and begins to use his talent as a lawyer on behalf of people on the streets in Washington, D.C. He begins to realize how much some people have invested in protecting their interests over helping the poorest of the poor, and he realizes that many of these folks are good people who deserve love and compassion as much as anyone else does. He begins to care, and it radically changes his life. It is significant that one of the things he has to give up in order to regain his compassion and his ability to love others is his dream of being a multi-million-dollar lawyer.

We face these same kinds of choices and decisions. Many people see suffering and need and choose to ignore it or walk away from it. If we wanted to pick on lawyers for just a few more minutes, we could look at the statistics that show that seventy percent of entering law students at Harvard "said they planned to practice public-interest law and that only about three percent ended up actually doing so."[8] (I'm not sure that I would want to see similar statistics showing the rate at which well-meaning clergy eventually end up serving things other than the God who originally called them into service.) Too often, we become numb to the desire that God has placed within us to do good. We tell ourselves that what would really make us happy is a new outfit or a new car or whatever it is that we think we need in order to be happy. When will we learn that we cannot buy or possess happiness?

Some people come up with an even more creative strategy to avoid doing good to others. They tell themselves they can't make a difference anyway. I have caught myself falling into this trap. But I have seen God's people make a difference through simple acts of faithfulness too many times to believe the lie that we cannot make a difference.

He Prayed for a Bicycle

I will never forget a young man I met on a short-term mission trip to Mexico. My group was building a casita (a small one-room house) for a family in a northern border town of Mexico. Our work was going very well. During one of my frequent breaks from working, I met a young man whom God used to touch my life. His name was Zacharias. I got to know Zacharias when I casually mentioned that I liked the cross he was wearing, and he took it off and gave it to me. I was stunned and humbled by his instinctive generosity.

During this particular trip, my small group had been plagued by a bicycle that someone from our church had donated for us to give away while we were in Mexico. It was constantly in the way. One night our group was especially tired, and we began to talk about how we could get rid of this bike. We did not have the best motivations; we just wanted to get rid of the bike that was annoying us because we kept bumping into it. We had put off taking the bike with us to the work site for several days because it wouldn't fit comfortably in the van with us. At our small-group meeting this particular night, I shared about meeting Zacharias, and someone in our group suggested that we give the bike to "that kid that gave Kevin the cross." (I don't want to make us look too good. In order to get the intended effect, you need to imagine someone mumbling this in a very tired voice who is interested in just ending the conversation. God was definitely working in spite of us!) We decided that this was the best way to finally get rid of the bike.

The next morning, we squeezed into our van and took turns complaining about how uncomfortable it was to have the bike with us. When we got to the work site, Zacharias showed up, but we almost forgot about the bike. Suddenly I remembered, and I asked our translator to tell him that we had brought something for him, and I went and got the bike out and gave it to him.

I have to admit I was surprised by his reaction. He didn't say anything. He just kind of blankly stared at the bike and asked a few questions of our translator, basically clarifying that this was actually being given to him. Then he rode off. Initially, I felt a bit disappointed. Maybe I was hoping at least to match my feeling when he had given me the cross the day before. Or maybe I was uncomfortable feeling as if I were in his debt. Or maybe I just wanted to get to see someone be really happy and excited, like the reaction a child has when he gets exactly what he asked Santa Claus for on Christmas morning.

We went back to work. Just as the event had almost completely left my mind, Zacharias came back. He looked embarrassed and was trying to find our translator. When we found her, Zacharias asked if we would come with him to his house. His mother wanted to speak to us. My first reaction was, oh great, I am in trouble for giving someone a bike!

At Zacharias' house, we discovered that his mom thought he had stolen the bike. When he insisted that he hadn't, she told him he better prove it. So he asked us to tell her that we had given him the bike. As soon as she realized what had happened, she became overwhelmed.

Through our translator I learned that Zacharias had been pestering his mom about getting a bike for quite some time, but they didn't have the money. He wanted the bike so that he could get a job after school and help support his family. In desperation, she told Zacharias to pray to God for a bike. She told us that she had told him to do that the night before! The next morning God gave Zacharias a bike. God used a group of grumbling missionaries to do it!

I wish I could convey to you the experience we had at Zacharias' house, how thick the air was with the presence of God. It was not magical, like when the dementors show up in a Harry Potter movie. It was simply one of the most humbling experiences of my life. It is the closest I have ever come to experiencing what it is like to want to take off your shoes because the place where you are standing is holy ground.

Though I know God was present and in control, I sometimes struggle with whether to tell this story because I know that God does not always answer our prayers in such adramatic fashion. I am not sharing this story to encourage you to pray for stuff so that you can have more things, but in order to show how God can use even our most flawed efforts to help in miraculous ways. Zacharias was not just praying for a new toy; he was praying for a way to help support his family. I don't know how the story ended, or what happened to Zacharias. We certainly did not solve all of his problems. But we did make a difference. The Lord works in mysterious ways.

Called To Make a Difference

As we think about loving our neighbors as ourselves, the challenge we face is not to attempt to solve all of the world's problems. Instead, I believe we are called to make what difference we can and look to God for strength and grace. We can start by fighting the instinct that we often have to protect ourselves and our stuff from others. We can work to bless others the way that God has blessed us. One of the major strengths behind early Methodism was that everyone was invested in doing these things. The General Rules were designed to help all Methodists actively practice their faith. No one was allowed to be a passive Christian.

The challenge we often face is not a willingness or desire to make a difference, but instead a paralyzing fear of failure. Often, those who sincerely want to make a difference simply don't know where to begin. I would like to conclude this chapter by offering a few suggestions on how we can focus our efforts today to do all the good that we can.

First, support your local church. In *The Scandal of the Evangelical Conscience* Ron Sider cites a study that revealed that "in 1968, the average church member gave 3.1 percent of his or her income . . . That figure dropped every year through 1990 and then recovered slightly to 2.66 percent."[9] We can do much better than that. I believe that Christians are called to give generously to benefit others. Christians can often feed the hungry, clothe the naked, and visit the sick simply by supporting their church and its ministries.

At the same time, individual congregations need to remember that it is every church's responsibility to be a good steward of the resources that are entrusted to them. Too many congregations spend almost all of the money that they collect on themselves. Many congregations have become so inwardly focused that they tend to develop a culture of scarcity rather than abundance. If you are a member of a congregation that is not faithfully using its resources to bless others, you may need to prayerfully consider how much money God is leading you to give to your local church and what other ways you can use the resources that you have been entrusted with to love others.

Second, support organizations that exist to serve groups with specific needs. The United Methodist Church, for instance, has recently participated in the Nothing But Nets campaign, which raises money to provide mosquito nets to protect Africans from malaria. A ten-dollar donation provides one family with a net and education on how to use it effectively. On Valentine's Day of 2008, Nothing But Nets had received donations for 1,821,256 nets! You can contribute to Nothing But Nets by visiting their website at http://nothingbutnets.net.

Another organization that my wife and I have supported is Blood:Water Mission. Their website says:

> This, then, is the Blood:Water Mission, committed to clean blood and clean water to fight the HIV/AIDS pandemic, to build clean wells in Africa, to support medical facilities caring for the sick, to make a lasting impact in the fight against poverty, injustice and oppression in Africa through the linking of needs, talents and continents, of people and resources.[10]

Blood:Water Mission is able to provide clean drinking water to one person for one year for just one dollar! It is heartbreaking to think of the number of God's children who do not have access to clean drinking water. I am thankful to have the opportunity to support a ministry that is doing all that it can to address this problem. You can contribute to Blood:Water Mission by visiting their website at www.bloodwatermisison.com.

The United Methodist Committee on Relief (UMCOR) is another excellent organization whose mission is "grounded in the teachings of Jesus . . . to alleviate human suffering—whether caused by war, conflict or natural disaster, with open hearts and minds to all people."[11] UMCOR is exceptional because it is one hundred percent efficient. All of the overhead and administrative costs of UMCOR are paid through the United Methodist apportionment system, so one hundred percent of every dollar you give to UMCOR is spent on the project you designate it for. You can learn more or contribute to UMCOR by visiting their website at http://new.gbgm-umc.org/umcor/.

Many other organizations are dedicated to doing "all the good that they can." From my perspective, the important thing is not to determine which one is perfect or where an organization falls short. Any organization can be improved. Sometimes we focus on the weaknesses, rather the strengths, of a group that is trying to do good to others. I encourage you to pray about where God is leading you to make a difference, and then do something!

A third way to "do good" is to go on a short-term mission trip. For many people, this is a very scary thing to do. It takes a leap of faith to go as an adult sponsor on a youth mission trip and spend hours stuck in a van with teenagers! (Or it may take a leap of faith to leave your home and your parents for a week for the first time.) However, getting out of our comfort zone and taking a risk is exactly what many American Christians desperately need. I have never had people tell me that they wished that they had not gone on a mission trip after it was over. And I have seen several people go on a trip kicking and screaming, but when they came back they choked up every time they tried to talk about it because it had been such a meaningful experience.

We do help others on short-term mission trips. However, the people who gain the most are often the ones who go. I have seen God work to open people's eyes to the humanity of people who are very different from themselves have when they enter into their lives to love and serve them, and to be served by them, even if it is only for a week. These trips teach us how to love others, and they show us how much God loves them and us.

My final suggestion for "doing all the good that you can" is to get to know the needs of people in your community. This is, in my mind, the most important of any of these suggestions. Our neighbors are watching us, and most of the time they see us loving and serving ourselves. I wonder if it would be easier for them to believe that God loves them if we loved them in the name of Jesus? It is a blessing to be able to give to organizations like Blood:Water Mission, Nothing But Nets, UMCOR, and to be able to go on short-term mission trips. But there is no substitute for getting to know the needs that people in your community have. Many churches have the resources to make a wonderful impact on their community. I get very excited thinking about the power that would be unleashed if members of every congregation commit together, as a community of faith, to doing all the good that they can right where they are.

May you step out in faith to love your neighbor as yourself. May you do all the good that you can. Jesus' commandment to love your neighbor as yourself is not intended to be a punishment. It is intended to help us live life as God intended. If this seems like an oppressive burden, think about the times that you have stepped out in faith to serve God. In my experience, every time people do this, they experience tremendous blessings and joy, not sorrow and regret. If you have never taken that kind of risk, maybe it is time to do so. Listen prayerfully to what God is leading you to do to love your neighbor, and then do it! God wants to use you to make a difference in someone else's life. Will you allow God to use you?

1. How are you currently living for what God has given you a burden or passion?

2. How do you find yourself trying to buy happiness?

3. How have you seen God move in ways similar to the story about my friend Zacharias?

4. Are you familiar with any of the organizations like Blood:Water Mission that are mentioned in this chapter? Do you support any other organizations that "do all the good that they can? Which ones?

5. How have you seen God at work through involvement with a short-term mission trip? If you haven't been on one, would you consider going on one? Why, or Why not?

6. What can you do in your community to do good to others?

7. What has God been calling you to do but you have been putting off doing? What steps can you take toward being faithful to God's calling?

Endnotes

1. This story was originally told by Loren Eiseley in his book *The Star Thrower* (New York: Times Books, 1978), 169-185.

2. *Methodist Societies,* "The Nature, Design, and General Rules of the United Societies," 9:72.

3. *Methodist Societies,* "The Nature, Design, and General Rules of the United Societies," 9:72.

4. *Methodist Societies,* "The Nature, Design, and General Rules of the United Societies," 9:72.

5. Matthew 25:31-40 (*TNIV*).

6. John Grisham, *The Street Lawyer* (New York: Island, 1998), 16.

7. Grisham, 19.

8. Brian J. Mahan, *Forgetting Ourselves on Purpose: Vocation and the Ethics of Ambitio,* (San Francisco: Jossey-Bass, 2002), 143-144.

9. Sider, 20.

10. <http://www.bloodwatermission.com/index.php?em1204=43910>, accessed Feb. 14, 2008.

11. <http://new.gbgm-umc.org/umcor/about/>, accessed Feb. 14, 2008.

The Third Rule:
Practice the Christian Disciplines

Practice, Practice, Practice

Practice makes perfect. Well, maybe not exactly. But it usually doesn't hurt. I learned the value of practice during my childhood when I fell in love with the game of baseball. Every year, I became increasingly passionate about baseball. I wanted to be the best baseball player I could be. I wanted to be good enough to play high school baseball, and maybe even college.

I learned two hard lessons from playing baseball that are probably true in many areas of life. First, I learned that people often judge you based on things other than your performance. When we moved just before baseball season began during my freshman year of high school, I learned that reputation matters. When we moved from Lafayette, Louisiana, to Edmond, Oklahoma, I did not get to take my reputation with me. The second thing I learned was that people judge you based on your appearance. When my family moved from Edmond to Houston, Texas, after living for a year and a half in Edmond, the varsity baseball coach in Houston told me I was too small. He told me that there was not a realistic chance that I would make the team.

At the time, I cared about baseball too much to let someone glance at me between classes with me in my school clothes and tell me I was not good enough. I decided to work as hard as I could to prove him wrong. Every day after school, my dad and I went to a baseball field in our neighborhood and practiced for at least an hour, sometimes two. I hit hundreds of balls and then traded my bat for a glove, and my dad hit grounders to me as hard as he could. It was hard work. But I loved it because I loved baseball.

Ultimately, all of my practice paid off, and I made the team. I still had something to prove, though, because I was told that I wouldn't ever get to play. I played second base, and they already had a second baseman. All I could do was keep working as hard as I could. Eventually, my opportunity came, and I took advantage of it. By the end of the season, I had earned the starting spot at second base. Looking back, I realize that all this practice did not guarantee me any success. But, I would have been guaranteed not to succeed if I had not put in hours and hours of practice.

The perseverance and work ethic I learned from practicing baseball with my dad were some of the most valuable lessons of my childhood. This experience it is one of the key things that shaped me into the person I am today. I learned how to stick with things that did not come easily right away. I also learned how to work hard in the face of adversity.

After playing baseball for many years, it was hard to give it up. By the time I played my last game, being a baseball player was one of the most important parts of my identity. If you had asked me when I was playing baseball during my freshman year of college at a Division III school what was most central to who I was, I would have said being a baseball player and a Christian. I am afraid it would have been in that order.

Based on the amount of time I spent playing or practicing baseball, this makes sense. I would guess I averaged three hours a day of playing baseball during my last year of high school and my first year of college. I might have averaged thirty minutes a day practicing and sharpening my faith.

Out of Proportion

Have you ever noticed how the things that we often get worked up about, the things we are most passionate about, are often not the same things that we say are the most important to us? Staying with the theme of baseball, we could consider the reaction to the recognition of widespread drug abuse by major league baseball players during the late 1990s and the first decade of the twenty-first century. In early 2008, there were hearings in the capital of the United States of America that lasted five hours where congressmen and women questioned Roger Clemens, one of the greatest pitchers in the history of baseball, and his former trainer Brian McNamee. McNamee had previously told prosecutors that he injected Roger Clemens on several occasions with steroids and Human Growth Hormone (HGH). Clemens has steadfastly denied ever using steroids or HGH.

This was deemed such a national emergency that the United States Congress decided to get involved. As a result, both Roger Clemens and Brian McNamee were placed under oath and were grilled by different members of the House of Representatives about who was telling the truth. As if to highlight the ridiculousness of the proceedings, one congressman asked what jersey Roger Clemens would wear into the Hall of Fame. As I watched part of the proceedings while eating lunch, I was appalled and embarrassed.

Watching Clemens and McNamee's testimony, it was easy to forget that this was about baseball, a game that is played for fun, to entertain people. Yet, ESPN carried the entire hearing without commercial interruption. An outside observer would be forgiven if he or she thought that America valued finding out whether or not Roger

Clemens was injected with steroids more highly than it valued finding a way to feed the millions of people who are starving to death. Or compare the proceedings with the importance of the continued violations of basic freedoms and human rights taking place in many parts of the world. Or how to improve education. Or what to do about the damage we are doing to the environment through our over-consumption. We seemed to put more energy into debating whether Roger Clemens' legacy was tainted by steroids than into debating how we can best use our national resources. Something is wrong.

American Christians need to learn to practice their faith with as much passion, energy, and dedication as they argue about who the best baseball player of all time is and whether it matters if he used performance-enhancing drugs. Here is a radical idea: Christians should practice their faith more passionately, more energetically, and with more dedication than they practice anything else. For Christians, practicing their faith should be the number-one priority in their lives.

Practicing Our Faith

So far, we have discussed the first two General Rules, which are "do no harm" and "do all the good that you can." The first General Rule reminds us that, before we can grow in our relationship with God, we have to stop doing things that cause us to move away from God's presence. The second rule reminds us to follow Jesus' command to love our neighbor as ourselves by doing all the good that we can. In this chapter, we will look at the third General Rule, which is essentially a reminder to practice our faith with passion and dedication.

In the General Rules, Wesley wrote, "It is expected of all who desire to continue in these societies that they should continue to evidence their desire of salvation, *Thirdly* by attending upon all the ordinances of God. Such are: The public worship of God; The ministry of the Word, either read or expounded; The Supper of the Lord; Family and private prayer; Searching the Scriptures; and Fasting, or abstinence."[1]

In the first General Rule, "do no harm," Wesley listed several specific things that we should not do. Some of them, such as not wearing enormous bonnets, seem outdated today. I have a feeling that his list might look a little bit different if he were coming up with a new one today. However, I would guess the list would be almost exactly the same today if Wesley were to come up with a new list for this third rule. Let's take a closer look at these essential Christian practices.

The first practice that Wesley mentions is the "public worship of God." This is as obvious as it sounds. Christians who are committed to their faiths will gather to worship God. According to *The Book of Discipline of the United Methodist Church*, local churches exist "for the maintenance of worship, the edification of believers, and the redemption of the world."[2] Maintaining the communal practice of worshipping God, then, is one of the fundamental things that any local church does. When a church ceases to maintain worship, that church is essentially dead and is no longer rightly considered a church.

This is so basic, yet how many people who consider themselves members of a church fail to consistently worship God with their family of faith? The early Methodists did not allow people who routinely neglected to come to worship to call themselves Methodists. Yet one of the most obvious signs of how low many congregations have set the bar for membership is the number of people who are still considered members, even though they have not darkened the doors of the church where they are "members" to worship for years!

Interestingly, Wesley added the word "public" as an adjective describing what kind of worship he was talking about. The primary place that Methodists worshipped God was in the society meetings, which would have been similar to a worship service today. Worshipping God with other believers was essential because it drew the faithful closer to God and to one another. In worship Methodists sang hymns, prayed, read scripture, heard sermons, and received the sacrament of Holy Communion (when there was an ordained pastor present). In one sense, then, worship was essential to discipleship because in worship a new follower was introduced to the other Christian practices. It was also important because it was a place where many people were introduced to the gospel and were awakened to their need for salvation.

Methodists were known for being particularly bold in their public proclamation of the gospel. Wesley often preached outdoors to crowds in the middle of the town. This style of preaching was known as "field preaching." Though Wesley did not always enjoy field preaching, he found it to be one of the primary ways people responded to the gospel message. Unfortunately, today we seem to express our faith in increasingly private, individualized ways, rather than publicly joining as the Body of Christ to worship our Lord. The reminder to practice "public worship of God" is as relevant and important as ever.

The second practice that Wesley mentions is "the ministry of the Word, either read or expounded." This is another practice that should be very familiar to most Christians. Wesley is referring to either reading scripture aloud in order to exhort, instruct, or build others up, or reading scripture and then "expounding" on it—in other words, preaching on a selected scripture passage. While many churches continue to give lip service to the importance of scripture, there seems to be an increase in biblical illiteracy in many congregations. The sermon also has a nearly sacred place in many worship services. But how often do people listen to a sermon and actually change an opinion or a behavior based on it? Wesley would be pleased that we continue to read and preach on the scriptures in our worship services, but he would want us to put what we are reading and being taught into practice in our lives.

The next practice that Wesley mentions is the "Supper of the Lord" or Holy Communion. Wesley referred to Holy Communion as the "grand channel whereby the grace of his Spirit was conveyed to the souls of all the children of God."[3] For Wesley and the early Methodists, Holy Communion represents the unending river of grace that we are invited to swim in every time we come to the Lord's table. It is ready and waiting for us.

The sacrament of Holy Communion is important to discipleship because it is the most obvious place where Christians can expect to encounter God's grace in tangible and life-changing ways. Communion, for Wesley, was one of the key practices that enabled one to grow in grace and become more holy. I think Wesley would be surprised and saddened by the reality that most United Methodist Churches offer Communion only once a month. Ultimately, the sacrament of Holy Communion is one of the cornerstones of the Wesleyan blueprint for discipleship.

In the third General Rule, the next thing Wesley mentions as an important Christian practice is "family and private prayer." Wesley's own prayer life was an astounding model of dedication, faithfulness, and perseverance. He woke up at 4:00 a.m. every morning and spent one hour on his knees in prayer and Bible reading. He did this again at night before he went to bed. I vividly remember visiting the house that Wesley lived in toward the end of his life in London, England. The room that Wesley slept in was modest, even sparse. Next to his room was a smaller room with a kneeling pad and a desk that had a large Bible on it. Standing in the same room where Wesley spent so many hours on his knees in prayer was a powerful and humbling experience for me.

Prayer does not need much of a defense. Most Christians would acknowledge the importance of prayer. It is an important Christian practice because prayer is the primary way that we communicate with God. When we pray, we bring our lives before God and listen for God's will for our lives. We bring our joys, concerns, hopes, fears, and every other part of our lives before God. Prayer is a particularly challenging discipline for some people because we often don't get the immediate results that we are used to getting in many of the other parts of our lives. For some, prayer can even be a frustrating and disappointing discipline when God does not respond quickly and unmistakably. Unfortunately, many people spend more time feeling guilty about not praying than they actually spend praying.

Prayer is best understood not as the time when we bring God our to-do lists, but rather as a conversation with God. Praying involves listening for God's guidance and direction, and seeking to be molded and shaped so that we become more and more like Christ. [4]

When I was in seminary, one of my professors invited my wife and me over for dinner one evening. They had three delightful, but very young, children. When it was time for them to go to bed, their parents invited Melissa and me to join in their time of family prayer. This was their nightly family practice. From that experience, I learned that one of the best ways to make prayer a habit is to pray together as a family. Praying with young children is one of the most chaotic things I have done, but it is also a wonderful, grace-filled experience. As Melissa and I drove home that night, we talked about how powerful it was to witness these children already beginning to cultivate a relationship with God. It was also powerful to experience the way that family prayer brought them even closer together.

After prayer, the next Christian practice in the third General Rule is "searching the scriptures." This practice involves reading the Bible in order to discover God's guidance and direction. It is interesting to note that Wesley made a distinction between the reading of scripture in the context of a worship service and personally spending time searching the scriptures. For Wesley, it was clearly not enough to go to church once a week and trust that you would learn all you needed to know about the Bible by hearing one or two short passages of scripture and a fifteen to thirty-minute sermon. Wesley expected Christians to search the scriptures on their own, and to read them seeking God's will and God's direction.

The scriptures were clearly a crucial focus in Wesley's approach to discipleship. In his preface to *Sermons on Several Occasions*, Wesley wrote, "I want to know one thing, the way to heaven—how to land safe on that happy shore. God himself has condescended to teach the way . . . . He hath written it down in a book. O give me that book! . . . I have it. Here is knowledge enough for me."[5] Thus, for Wesley, searching the scriptures meant reading the Bible not just to gain information, but also to be transformed. This way of reading the Bible involved seeking God's direction and wisdom and putting what was learned into practice immediately. Searching the scriptures is important to discipleship, then, because it is the primary place where one finds guidance for how to live as a disciple of Jesus Christ. Just as it is not controversial to suggest that Christians should spend time in prayer, it is not likely to stir up controversy to suggest that Christians should read the Bible. However, saying that it is important and actually doing it can be very different things.

Finally, Wesley lifts up "fasting or abstinence" as important Christian practices. Fasting is the practice of not eating food for a period of time. Wesley regularly fasted throughout his life, either once or twice a week. Abstinence refers to abstaining from something. For many people, sexual intercourse is the first thing that comes to mind. However, there are many other things that we can abstain from for a period of time in order to focus on our relationship with God. Some people commonly practice some form of abstinence during the season of Lent. The point of fasting and abstinence is not to make ourselves miserable. Instead, it is a means of reminding us of our dependence on God. Fasting from food, for example, reminds us that we are dependent on God and that life itself is a gift. Fasting can also serve as a call to prayer. When we fast, our hunger serves as a reminder to pray for the ability to be faithful. Successfully fasting or abstaining from something also provides concrete evidence that we can make our flesh submit to our will and our desire to follow God.

We could discuss other Christian practices. Wesley believed that individual Christians should include those disciplines that they found particularly helpful to them in their relationship with God. The point is to do those things that help us grow in our faith and our commitment to God. It is important to keep these Christian practices in mind so that other things don't distract us and cause us to lose sight of our priorities. These Christian practices help us synchronize what we say are the most important things with how we actually live our lives and spend our time and our money. All three General Rules, in fact, are ways to keep us focused, to help keep our eyes on Jesus.

Peter learned, when he walked on water, that it was crucial to keep his eyes on Jesus. Similarly, if we neglect these practices, we will begin to look to other things, and we will start to sink. But if we practice our faith with passion, seeking to come to know God's love more and more deeply, we will find that with the passage of time we will get better at keeping our eyes on Jesus in the midst of the storms of life.

If we commit ourselves to "do no harm," "do all the good that we can," and "practice the spiritual disciplines," we will find that we are beginning to follow Jesus' commandment to love God and love our neighbor. We will find that we are cooperating with God's sanctifying grace, which makes us more and more like Jesus himself. We will find that practicing these habits of holiness works to allow God into our lives to make us holy. We will become the kind of people who not only call ourselves Christians, but also have a living, active, and vigorous faith. This is a faith that the world will notice and for which it hungers.

—— Questions for Discussion ——

1. How are the things that excite you consistent with the things that you say are the most important priorities in your life? What inconsistencies are there between the two?

2. What Christian practices are you currently doing? Which of these are you the most comfortable with? Why?

3. Which Christian practices do you find to be the most difficult to do? Why?

4. Is there a Christian practice that you have not been in the habit of doing, but that would help you grow in your love of God and neighbor? What is it? Would you be willing to commit to start practicing it? Who will hold you accountable?

Endnotes

1. *Methodist Societies,* "The Nature, Design, and General Rules of the United Societies," 9:73.

2. *The Book of Discipline of the United Methodist Church* (Nashville: The United Methodist Publishing House, 2004), 127.

3. *Sermons,* "Upon our Lord's Sermon on the Mount: Discourse the Sixth," 1:585.

4. For further guidance on the practice of prayer see: Richard Foster, *Prayer: Finding the Heart's True Home* (San Francisco: Harper, 1992); and Robert Benson, *In Constant Prayer* (Nashville: Thomas Nelson, 2008).

5. *Sermons* "Preface," 1:105.

7

Finding the Balance

The Balance Point

During the only year that I played college baseball, I realized that I was not going to get much playing time in the position I had the most experience playing, second base. I decided to try to earn some playing time as a pitcher. I did not have any previous experience pitching, so I had to start at the beginning. I taught myself the basics of pitching by trying to remember what I had heard past coaches say to the pitchers on my old teams. One of the first things that I focused on was the mechanics of the windup, or the motion that a pitcher goes through in order to build momentum and rhythm with the hope of achieving increased speed and accuracy.

One of the primary sources of information I had about pitching came from my experience as a high-school baseball player teaching a baseball camp for little-league kids. I remember our coaches teaching these ten-year-olds that the key part of the windup, or pitching delivery, was the balance point. We called the balance point the scarecrow, because that is what it looked like. But in order to be the best possible pitcher, it is necessary to be able to find the balance point and then be able to hold it. We instructed the kids to hold this position for up to a minute in order to make sure they mastered it. The balance point was important because we knew that if a pitcher fell backward, he or she would lose accuracy and velocity, and the pitch would be too high. Or, if the pitcher fell forward, he or she would again lose accuracy and velocity, and the pitch would usually be too low. I realized that if I wanted to become a good pitcher, the first thing I had to do had nothing to do with throwing a baseball; it had to do with finding the balance point.

In the previous three chapters, we have discussed the three General Rules that Wesley instituted in early Methodism to help Methodists grow in holiness of heart and life. Since making disciples of Jesus Christ is the mission of the United Methodist Church, we can learn from the General Rules. The first rule is "do no harm," or do nothing that leads you away from God. The idea is that you cannot move forward until you stop going backward. The second rule is to "do all the good that you can." We looked at Jesus' command to "love our neighbor as ourselves" and the expectation in scripture that followers of Jesus will feed the hungry, clothe the naked, and visit those who are sick and in prison. The third and final General Rule, "Attend upon the ordinances of God," is an old-fashioned way of saying, "Practice the instituted means of grace." The spiritual disciplines, or Christian practices, include the public worship of God, the ministry of the Word of God, family and private prayer, the Lord's Supper, searching the scriptures, and fasting. The third rule is a way to obey the first part of Jesus' commandment to "Love God with all our heart, soul, mind, and strength." Thus,.the General Rules offer a blueprint for how Christians can obey the teachings of Jesus and become deeply committed.

The Right Kind of Balance

One of the major benefits of committing to live by the General Rules is that it can help us find balance in our lives. Just like any good pitcher, if we want to stay on track in our journeys with Christ, it is important to find the balance point. In a time when people are juggling more activities and responsibilities than ever before, surely we could all use a little more balance.

Before we go any farther, we need to make sure that we are all on the same page when we talk about balance. There are some ways of talking about balance that are consistent with the teachings of Jesus, and there are other ways of talking about balance that work as a defense mechanism and protect us from really having to decide whether we will follow Jesus. Consider Jesus' exhortation in Mark 8:34-38:

> Whoever wants to be my disciple must deny themselves and take up their cross and follow me. For whoever wants to save their life will lose it, but whoever loses their life for me and for the gospel will save it. What good is it for you to gain the whole world, yet forfeit your soul? Or what can you give in exchange for your soul? If any of you are ashamed of me and my words in this adulterous and sinful generation, the Son of man will be ashamed of you when he comes in his Father's glory with the holy angels.

I want to be clear. If you take what I am saying as an opportunity to seek "balance" in your life between church and entertainment or other things, then you are misunderstanding me. In fact, I want to encourage you as strongly as I can to make sure that Christ is the number-one priority in your life.

What balance, then, are we trying to find? We are trying to find balance within the Christian life, not balance between the Christian life and something else. Throughout the centuries, Christians have tended to move back and forth between different extremes. One extreme lifts up faith to the total exclusion of works, while the other extreme views works as a means of earning salvation. Emphasizing either faith or works, to the exclusion of the other, oversimplifies the Christian message. The result of lifting up faith to the exclusion of works is often passive Christians whose lives are more obviously faithful to the broader culture than they are to the way of life of the gospel. Faith without works leads to a watered-down form of Christianity that creates cultural Christians who are practically atheists.

On the other hand, lifting up works to the exclusion of faith in the power and work of Jesus Christ tends to produce self-sufficient Christians who are unable to recognize their need to be saved by someone outside of themselves. A result of this oversimplification is that people desperately work to earn their salvation. They try to become "good" so that God will accept them. Works in the absence of faith in Jesus Christ and the grace that comes through him results in people who are really trying to save themselves.

In the General Rules, Wesley provides a powerful solution to the tension between faith and works. Much as a pitcher needs to find his or her balance point in order to be able to throw strikes consistently, the General Rules help us to find a balance that enables us to affirm both the scriptural emphasis on salvation by grace through faith and the reality that faith without works is dead. In other words, the most faithful articulation of the gospel is one that highlights who Jesus is and what he has done in order to free us from slavery to sin and death, while simultaneously affirming that Jesus invites us into a new way of living. Jesus is not asking us simply to accept a ticket to heaven. Rather, Jesus is inviting us to receive the gift of new life.

Three Balance Points

In the remainder of this chapter, we will consider three different tensions, or misunderstandings, and we will look at how we can use the General Rules as a tool to help us find the appropriate balance. The three tensions we will consider are: faith vs. works; personal piety vs. social action; and love of God vs. love of neighbor. When Christians have tried to pick sides in these conflicts, inevitably they have strayed from the mark. They have overemphasized one part of the Christian faith and underemphasized another part of the Christian faith. In each case, the General Rules help Christians avoid the typical either/or response that many people have when confronted with these tensions. Instead, the General Rules lead Christians toward a both/and response that affirms the scriptural aspect of each.

Faith and Works

We have already said something about the first of these tensions, faith vs. works. I hope it has been clear that I am not arguing that one of these is scriptural and the other is not. Rather, my argument is that the reason there is a tension is that both concepts exist in scripture. If we attempt to force ourselves to resolve this tension by choosing one, faith or works, we end up emphasizing one part of the witness of scripture too strongly, while trying to minimize or ignore another part of the witness of scripture.

In Ephesians 2:8-9, for instance, we read, "It is by grace that you have been saved, through faith—and this is not from yourselves, it is the gift of God—not by works, so that no one can boast." This passage, and others like it, certainly lifts up the important role that faith plays in our salvation. John Wesley affirmed the importance of the role of faith. In his sermon, "Justification by Faith," Wesley wrote, "Faith . . . is the *necessary* condition of justification . . . the *only necessary* condition."[1] Wesley tried to remind members of his own church (the Church of England) of their own foundation on justification by faith by quoting "the words of our own Church." Wesley tried to call Christians back to the belief that "the only instrument of salvation... is faith . . . a sure trust and confidence . . . that God both hath and will forgive our sins, that he hath accepted us again into his favour... for the merits of Christ's death and Passion."[2]

At times, Christians have emphasized the importance of justification by faith so strongly that they have excluded any role for works or participation in our own salvation. People have sometimes even been condemned for trying to do anything to "earn" their salvation. During Wesley's lifetime, this was a particular danger. Some of the early Methodists moved away from Wesley toward a group of Moravian Christians who practiced Quietism, which taught that there was literally nothing that anyone could do to contribute to his own salvation. Thus, once people were awakened to their need for forgiveness by grace through faith in Jesus Christ, they were instructed to do nothing but wait quietly for God to give the gift of faith. This was a position that Wesley and those who remained a part of the Methodist movement repudiated.

Imagine waking up to the reality that you were headed to hell, and away from the presence of God, and then being told that you could do nothing but wait! It would be like someone telling you that you had cancer and then telling you simply to wait patiently for a cure, even though there were already several different options for effective treatment. Wesley believed that people should practice the spiritual disciplines in order to participate with the work that God's grace was trying to do in their lives. And as strongly as Ephesians 2:8-9 emphasizes the importance of faith, the very next verse sheds positive light on the role that works plays in the Christian life: "For we are God's handiwork, created in Christ Jesus to do good works, which God prepared in advance for us to do."

The case for works is often made by appealing to James 2:14-17:

> What good is it, my brothers and sisters, if people claim to have faith but have no deeds? Can such faith save them? Suppose a brother or sister is without clothes and daily food. If one of you says to them, "Go in peace; keep warm and well fed," but does nothing about their physical needs, what good is it? In the same way, faith by itself, if it is not accompanied by action, is dead.

This passage, and others like it, points clearly to the expectation that Christian faith leads to action. There seems to be a clear emphasis in scripture on the role of "work[ing] out your salvation with fear and trembling."[3] Wesley clearly understood the importance of practicing what you preach. Wesley used the phrase "means of grace" to refer to the things that Christians could do in order to expect to grow in holiness. Wesley defined the means of grace as "outward signs, words, or actions ordained of God, and appointed for this end—to be the *ordinary* channels whereby he might convey to men preventing [or prevenient], justifying, or sanctifying grace."[64] As such, the Christian practices mentioned in the third General Rule are essential means of grace. More generally, we understand the General Rules as a means of grace for Christians. Christians have also understood "working out your salvation" as fulfilling Jesus' double commandment to love God and neighbor. As a result, it is doing those things that cause us to love and serve our neighbors, as well as doing the things that cause us to grow in our love and knowledge of God.

Works are important. However, some Christians have tended to overemphasize works at the expense of faith. This overemphasis forgets that salvation is truly a gift of God and we can do nothing to force God's hand. This perspective struggles to recognize that we are fallen people who need to be saved and that we cannot save ourselves. Only God can save us. Many Christians today seem to forget about God's amazing grace and the love that God freely pours on us. This love empowers us and makes it possible for us to respond. Wesley's understanding of grace provides a helpful reminder that salvation is a gift that comes to us when we are unable to save ourselves. The General Rules provide a blueprint that, if we follow it, will help us to avoid presuming upon God's grace and living as if we were not children of God. In other words, the General Rules help us practice the faith that has been graciously given to us.

Personal Piety and Social Action

The Wesleyan blueprint for discipleship also helps us to maintain balance between personal piety and social action. If we agree that both faith and works are important, then we might logically ask, "Which works?" In other words, what should followers of Jesus Christ do in order to grow in their faith? Looking back to Jesus' double commandment to love God and neighbor, we see that scripture lifts up the importance of doing both things that are an expression of love for God and an expression of love for neighbor.

Christians, however, have fallen into the trap of either emphasizing personal piety at the expense of works of mercy or justice, or emphasizing works of mercy or justice at the expense of personal piety. When Christians overemphasize personal piety, they tend to focus on the individual's relationship with Jesus Christ but do not pay sufficient attention to the role that we are called to play within the Body of Christ. On the other hand, those within the church who have focused on the importance of works of mercy and social justice have often overemphasized mercy while underemphasizing or ignoring the importance of a personal relationship with God in Jesus Christ. Christians must remember that Jesus commanded his followers to do both. Scripture invites us to embrace a personal relationship with God, but followers of Jesus Christ are also commanded to "love their neighbor as themselves." Unfortunately, Christians have often overemphasized one at the expense of the other.

Wesleyan discipleship considers a faithful response to the love of God shown to us in Christ Jesus to be one that combines both works of piety and works of mercy. Discipleship based on a Wesleyan understanding of spirituality remembers that Jesus commanded his followers to work out their salvation by loving God and their neighbor. People often express love of God through works of piety such as praying and searching the scriptures. On the other hand, Christians express love of neighbor through what Wesley defines as works of mercy, including feeding the hungry and clothing the naked. Both works of piety and works of mercy play important roles in Wesleyan discipleship.

Unfortunately, the tension between personal piety and social action has become increasingly political. Many Christians bristle at the mention of social justice, seeing it as a liberal agenda divorced from genuine faith in Jesus Christ. Some Christians, on the other hand, have become very cynical of any talk about "me and Jesus." This reaction often suggests that personal piety is a thinly veiled excuse to avoid caring about the poor and the oppressed.

Instead of labeling either of these approaches in a way that is divisive to Body of Christ, Christians from both sides of this issue would do well to take a closer look at what the scriptures actually teach. If we take this task seriously, we will find that there are good reasons that some people passionately defend the need to cultivate a personal relationship with God, while others adamantly insist that personal faith that does not reach out to the poor and oppressed is faith that is dead. In other words, both sides are right! Personal piety and social action are both vital parts of Christian discipleship, and they are both clearly found in scripture.

The Wesleyan approach to discipleship provides an important contribution, then, because it provides an example of how to bridge the scriptural emphasis on personal piety and social action.

Love of God and Love of Neighbor

The Wesleyan blueprint for discipleship also helps disciples of Jesus Christ find the balance between love of God and love of neighbor. Because Jesus explicitly said that the two highest priorities for his followers were to love God and love their neighbor, it is not difficult to argue for the importance of loving both God and neighbor. This final balance may be the least controversial of the three. However, the tendency to overemphasize either love of God or love of neighbor relates to our tendency to lift up personal piety or social action at the expense of the other.

In other words, if our Christian practice tends to focus on our relationship with God but is blind to the lives of those around us, we would not only forget to balance our discipleship with social action, but we would also make the mistake of neglecting to love our neighbor as ourselves. Love of God and love of neighbor are intimately connected. If we love God, we must love our neighbors as God loves them (1 John 4:20).

The bad news may be that this causes many of us to recognize that we have not followed Jesus as faithfully as we may have thought. On the other hand, the good news is that most Christians are willing to admit that they should follow Jesus' instructions to love God and neighbor. These greatest commandments have enormous potential to help us emphasize both piety and mercy, or personal and social holiness.

One of the greatest strengths of the General Rules is that they provide a straightforward approach for how to follow Jesus and live the kind of life that Christ calls his followers to live. The first General Rule exhorts us to stop doing things that hinder our growth. If we harm our relationships with God or our neighbor, we are moving backwards. To put it negatively, the first General Rule exhorts us to stop violating the greatest commandment. The second General Rule encourages followers of Jesus Christ to do good to others. Wesley is simply trying to teach his followers to "love their neighbor as themselves." Finally, the third General Rule encourages followers of Jesus to develop and strengthen their relationship with God through Christian disciplines such as prayer, searching the scriptures, partaking of the Lord's Supper, worshipping God, and fasting.

Now that we have looked at each of the General Rules and considered how they help us keep a healthy balance in our lives with God, we can look again to the teachings of Jesus in order to recognize how firmly the Methodist blueprint for discipleship is grounded in scripture. Consider again Jesus' words in Matthew's Gospel:

> Hearing that Jesus had silenced the Sadducees, the Pharisees got together. One of them, an expert in the law, tested him with this question: "Teacher, which is the greatest commandment in the law?"

Jesus replied: "'Love the Lord your God with all your heart and with all your soul and with all your mind.' This is the first and greatest commandment. And the second is like it: 'Love your neighbor as yourself.' All the law and the prophets hang on these two commandments."[5]

The final piece that remains for putting the blueprint into practice is a method of support, encouragement, and accountability to bring the General Rules to life in our lives. Wesley created a system of organization where Methodists "watched over one another in love" with this very purpose in mind. We will turn our attention to the importance of communal support and encouragement in the next chapter.

Questions for Discussion

1. How are you doing with finding balance in your life? How are your priorities being reflected through the way that you spend your time and your money?

2. Why is it important to find balance between faith and works? Do you tend to overemphasize one or the other? Which one? How so?

3. Why is it important to find balance between personal piety and social action? Do you tend to overemphasize either works of piety or works of mercy? Which one? How can you work to find the balance between them?

4. Why is it important to find balance between expressing love of God and love of neighbor? How can the General Rules help you find balance between love of God and neighbor?

Endnotes

1. *Sermons*, "Justification by Faith," 1:196.
2. *Sermons*, "Justification by Faith," 1:195.
3. Philippians 2:12 (*TNIV*).
4. *Sermons*, "The Means of Grace," 1:381.
5. Matthew 22:34-40 (*TNIV*).

8

Watching Over One Another in Love: The Importance of Christian Community

Don't Try This at Home

In this chapter, we will discuss the early Methodist practice of "watching over one another in love" and its continuing relevance for the church today. The practice of "watching over one another in love" was the key piece that Wesley believed would bring the General Rules to life. Unfortunately, it has become very difficult to talk about accountability because that word has come to carry so much baggage of judgment and condemnation. Maybe it would be helpful to start by offering an example of what "watching over one another in love" does not look like.

At the end of my sophomore year of college, several of my closest friends and I decided to go away for a weekend of male bonding. We did the stereotypical thing that men often do when they are bonding; we headed out into the wilderness, leaving civilization behind.

On the second day of our trip, my best friend Andy and I decided to leave the security of the campsite and head out into the unknown. We each borrowed someone else's bike, and we were off in search of adventure. Unfortunately, I was not as good of a bike rider as I thought I was—not even close. I was also stupid. See, what we were really looking for were things to jump the bikes off of. We wanted to get airborne. We wanted to see if we could fly. We searched and searched to no avail until we found the perfect bump that was just smooth enough to go over and just big enough to be able to really pull up on the handle bars and get some air. There was even a hill leading down to it that allowed us to pedal furiously and get what turned out to be way too much speed.

Andy is a lot smarter than I am. He sized all this up and said, "I think I'll wait and see how it turns out when you do it." So I said: "I'll see you on the other side of biking immortality!" Unfortunately, I failed to realize how similar biking immortality is to biking mortality. Anyway, I went up to the very top of the hill and poured it on, coming down as fast as I could. I hit the bump and was flying. Once I was hurtling blissfully through the air, two things occurred to me. First, I was way too high, and I was going way too fast. Second, there wasn't really very much ground on the other side of the bump that I was jumping off of—probably fifty feet—and then a cliff that had a six to ten-foot drop.

At the same time that I realized this, Andy realized there was no way that I was not going to go over the cliff, so he began running after me. To make things even worse, I didn't know that if you lock up your brakes in midair, your tires will not stop faster; they will actually just bounce because they can't roll. And that is exactly what they did. Then, as Andy anticipated, I went flying off the cliff, completely out of his sight. The bad news is you could see a dent in the ground where some part of my body, I think my shoulder, smashed into the ground. The good news is that by the grace of God I lived to use the story of my stupidity as an illustration for this book!

This story illustrates how not to watch over one another in love.

If Andy and I had been watching over one another in love, Andy would never have let me do something so foolish! (Actually, as I recall it, he did his best to talk me out of it, and he came to my rescue as fast as he could. Andy is the kind of friend everybody would be lucky to have.) In all seriousness, the worst part of the story is that I was not wearing a helmet. I am very lucky that I was not seriously injured that day. If my friends and I had been watching over one another in love, they would never have let me get on a bike without wearing a helmet.

Don't Go It Alone

In hindsight, this story is a humorous anecdote. However, it also serves to illustrate an important principle in biking that relates to the Wesleyan understanding of watching over one another in love. In mountain biking, there are two very basic rules that you need to follow. If you follow these two rules, no matter what happens, they almost guarantee your survival. The first rule is always, always, always wear a helmet! Statistically, the only reason people die while mountain biking is that they are not wearing a helmet. The second rule is never, never, never go mountain biking alone! If you wear a helmet, you are not going to die, but that doesn't mean your chain won't break, or you won't hit a tree and break your arm, or you won't have a flat tire. All of these things have happened to me, well, except, miraculously, I never did break any bones. When you bike with someone else, you share the burden of carrying the tools and supplies that you need, and you dramatically increase the odds that one of you will be able to go back for help if the other one should fall and become seriously injured.

At first glance, the Christian life may not appear to be nearly as dangerous as mountain biking. That isn't necessarily true. When Christians try to go it alone, they are on dangerous ground. When we go it alone, we quickly and easily lose perspective. We can experience a loss of clarity. We can forget what it is that is unique about Christians. When we are living in isolation, we can (and usually will) compromise our faith and allegiance to the gospel for the sake of comfort.

Wesley was passionate about the need for Christians to "watch over one another in love" through small-group accountability. He does not mention small-group accountability explicitly in any of the three General Rules, but that is simply because small-group accountability was the foundation that the General Rules were built on. In the beginning of the General Rules, Wesley tells the story of how eight to ten people came to him in London seeking to grow in their faith. Wesley reports, "to these . . . I gave those advices from time to time which I judged most needful for them; and as always we concluded our meeting with prayer suited to their several necessities." In telling this story, Wesley writes:

> This was the rise of the United Society. . . . Such a Society is no other than "a company of men 'having the form, and seeking the power of godliness,' united in order to pray together, to receive the word of exhortation, and to watch over one another in love, that they may help each other to work out their salvation."[1]

This method of "watching over one another in love" was the foundation, the bedrock, of Wesleyan discipleship. Whenever people came to Wesley and said, "We have come to have faith in Jesus Christ as our Lord and savior. What do we do now," the first thing Wesley did was to place them in small groups where they would be taught the basics of Christian faith and life and helped to grow in holiness.

For Wesley, stagnation was impossible in the Christian life. You were either moving forward and growing in holiness, or you were moving backward and falling away from God. One of the most powerful ways that God's Spirit moved within the early Methodist movement was through this system of small group accountability and support for holiness of heart and life. God seems to have powerfully blessed our spiritual forebears as they came together for support and encouragement to grow in their faith. Methodism in general seemed to grow in holiness as individual Methodists came together in groups and made themselves vulnerable to each other because of their commitment to love God and neighbor. Wesley saw from experience that when Christians were left to go it alone, more often than not they fell away from the grace that they had received. (Remember from chapter three Wesley's evaluation of what was happening in Pembrokeshire in 1763 where the "awakened" were not being joined together. Wesley reported, with horror, "that nine in ten of the once awakened are now faster asleep than ever.")

Throughout the Methodist revival, Wesley found that when Christians joined together in the accountability structure that he organized, they tended to grow in holiness. However, if they tried to go it alone, they usually lost their zeal for loving God and for loving their neighbors as themselves. Over time, they began to live increasingly like the rest of the world instead of living as Jesus Christ called them to live.

Getting Back to Our Roots

Small-group accountability is the thread that ties all the pieces of Wesleyan discipleship together. Without the practice of meeting together in small groups, Methodists have tended to decrease in their zeal and determination to grow in holiness. In his lifetime, Wesley found that when Methodists joined together and talked about their spiritual lives, they consistently grew in their ability to love God and neighbor. When they did not do this, they fell away from practicing their faith. The decline of Methodism has often been connected to the removal of the class meeting as a requirement for membership in Methodist churches.

Being a Methodist used to entail participating in the method of going to worship weekly and also meeting in a small group to talk about practicing one's faith through works of mercy and works of piety. In small groups, Methodists sought to stay connected to God's grace, and they reminded each other that they could not do this on their own. Today, however, we have moved so far away from this method that many Methodists have a deep mistrust of accountability, fearing that it is judgmental and condemning. Many Methodists now think that nobody else has a right to ask them how they are doing spiritually. Nobody else has any business asking them if they are reading the Bible daily, praying, avoiding making excuses for going to worship, or consistently doing those things that encourage them to "work out their salvation."

In many ways, Methodists, and many other believers, have settled for a least common denominator faith where we don't want to offend anyone or expect too much. As a result, we have not offended people enough who call themselves Christians but refuse to be obedient to the basic tenets of Christian faith. We have not asked people to commit themselves in a meaningful way to living out their faith. I am convinced that the Wesleyan practice of "watching over one another in love" still has a major contribution to make to the contemporary United Methodist Church and to the broader church. We also need to remember that small-group accountability is not merely having a Bible study or going through any program or study. Instead, it involves talking to one another about where we are in our walk with the Lord. It involves asking each other if we are practicing our faith. Are we moving closer to God or farther away?

The idea is actually to live into the kind of Christian practice that we find in scripture. In Ephesians 4:14-16, Paul reveals the level of maturity that Christians can find when they "watch over one another in love":

> Then we will no longer be infants, tossed back and forth by the waves, and blown here and there by every wind of teaching and by the cunning and craftiness of people in their deceitful scheming. Instead, speaking the truth in love, we will in all things grow up into him who is the head, that is, Christ. From him the whole body, joined and held together by every supporting ligament, grows and builds itself up in love, as each part does its work.[2]

Our growth as disciples of Jesus Christ relates to our willingness to speak the truth in love to our brothers and sisters in Christ. I am not suggesting that this is easy. In fact, it takes a great deal of sensitivity and effort. However, we cannot go it alone and become faithful disciples of Jesus Christ. We are encouraged—in fact, we are called—to grow up and to follow the example of Jesus as we become increasingly Christ-like.

In some ways, "watching over one another in love" is not nearly as difficult as it may initially seem to be. A recent adaptation of the Methodist class meeting is Covenant Discipleship, which helps a group form a covenant that they will meet weekly and be mutually accountable to one another. The covenant includes acts of compassion, worship, justice, and devotion.[3]

Appendix B in this book also provides a guide for using this study in a small group. This guide is intended to be used beyond the study of the book itself. Once the book is completed, the group can continue to meet by omitting the time of discussion related specifically to the book and instead sharing with one another the responses to the question, "How is it with your soul?" Small groups often miss the opportunity to go deeper because they believe that a legitimate small group must gather for the purposes of going through a study that teaches them something. However, for many Christians, gathering together for prayer and discussion of how God has been at work in their lives would be more fruitful than another meeting that focuses on information and not transformation. Too often a group study of a book can be a hindrance to intimacy and will leave no one changed. On the other hand, "watching over one another in love" involves precisely a decision by a group to invest in one another's lives so that each person will grow in holiness.

Wesley defined Methodists during his life as people who "unite together to encourage and help each other in . . . working out [their] salvation, and for that end watch over one another in love."[4] This is a concept that many of us seem afraid of, or at least are slow to embrace. Why? Why wouldn't we want to be a people who are known for encouraging and helping each other to grow in faith, to experience all the blessings that God has for our lives? We live in a time when people do not seem to need to hear the gospel. Most non-Christians can tell you the basic message of Jesus' death for our sins. However, few people have seen the gospel lived. Wesleyan spirituality casts a vision that is big enough to live into in order to witness to the world how great our God is and what kind of community is possible because of the amazing grace offered to everyone by the God we worship as Father, Son, and Holy Spirit.

I believe that if we embrace this vision, we will remember that we don't need to reach out to others because we are tired or because we are declining in numbers and we need new lives to preserve our institutions. Instead, we will reach out to others because we really believe that we have something to offer that is of infinite and eternal value. We have something that is good news, something that we are blessed to be the stewards of, and we will want to freely and boldly offer this gospel (which means good news!) to all the world. We offer this good news, not because we want something from others, but because of a deep conviction that we have something they need in to live life as God intends. Living life to the fullness that God intends is, after all, what the Wesleyan blueprint for discipleship is all about!

Questions for Discussion

1. When have you tried going it alone in your Christian walk? How did this affect your growth in holiness over this period?

2. Why are Christians who go it alone more likely to compromise their faith for the sake of comfort than do those who are members of an accountability group?

3. How does the Wesleyan idea of "watching over one another in love" change your understanding of small-group accountability?

4. Why is stagnation in the Christian life impossible? What role does small-group accountability play in encouraging Christians to grow in their faith?

5. What experiences have you had with a small group where the members "watched over one another in love?" How could a group you are a member of incorporate an element of accountability? If you are not currently involved with a group like this, how could you become involved in one?

Endnotes

1. *Methodist Societies*, "The Nature, Design, and General Rules of the United Societies," 9:69.
2. Ephesians 4:14-16 (*TNIV*).
3. For more information on how to start a Covenant Discipleship, see Gayle Turner Watson, *Guide for Covenant Discipleship Groups* (Nashville: Discipleship Resources, 2001); or visit the General Board of Discipleship's website on Covenant Discipleship at http://www.gbod.org/smallgroup/cd/.
4. *Methodist Societies*, "Advice to the People Called Methodists," 9:125.

9

Where Are You Going?

Lost or Found?

I will never forget watching the Houston Astros, my favorite major league baseball team, play at the Astrodome. Everything about the Astrodome was huge. It was such an impressive structure when it first opened in 1965 that people often referred to it as the eighth wonder of the world.

The Astrodome itself wasn't the only thing that was on a large scale. There was an amazing amount of parking surrounding the stadium. There were posts with information on them to help you remember where you had parked, because if you forgot where you parked, you might never find your car again!

I should know.

One day, I went to an Astros game with my dad and brother. We were all very excited to get to watch the Astros play. We parked and walked through the parking lot to the Astrodome. We were so excited to be there that we didn't realize how far we had to walk to get to our seats. And when the game was over, my dad and I had different recollections about where our car was. My dad started going one way, and I said, "Where are you going?" I don't remember exactly what he said, but it was probably something obvious like, "To the car." I was pretty sure that our car was on the third-base side of the stadium, but my dad knew it was on the first-base side. Parents usually win those kinds of disagreements, so off we went towards the parking lots on the first-base side of the field.

In all honesty, we probably neither one really knew where the car was. And as Yogi Berra has said, "You've got to be very careful if you don't know where you're going, because you might not get there."[1] As we looked for the car, there definitely came a point where we did not know where we were going, and we began to wonder if we were ever going to get there. Our saving grace was that the parking lot began to empty out. Even this was a bit unsettling, because the only thing that makes the Astrodome's parking lot feel even bigger is when you are standing in the middle of it trying to find your car.

Just think how much more easily we would have found our car if we had simply remembered which section we had parked in!

Moving Toward Faithful Discipleship

A basic goal of this book has been to provide a blueprint that we can follow today with the hope that we will grow in our faith in Christ and in our ability to love God and our neighbor. If we don't know where we are going, we might not get there. I am afraid that many Christians do not know where they are going, and as a result, they never get there. I have argued that our destination, or goal, as Christians is holiness of heart and life. We are trying to become followers of Jesus Christ in actions as well as in words.

I have also presented the General Rules as a helpful blueprint for how the first Methodists arrived at this destination. I have argued that this same blueprint has enormous potential for us today. The blueprint for Wesleyan discipleship consists of two levels, or pillars. The first level in following the General Rules is to do no harm, to do all the good that we can, and to practice the spiritual disciplines. The second level involves "watching over one another in love" through a small-group accountability structure. These two levels are intimately connected. A major part of Wesley's genius was his realization that Christians were more likely to practice their faith (which was the basic goal of the General Rules) if they "watched over one another in love." If we follow this two-tiered structure, we will be on our way to becoming disciples of Jesus Christ. We will become people who have a robust, inspirational faith that will make a difference in our lives and will positively impact the lives of those we come into contact with.

Decision Time

I will conclude this book by pressing each of us to make a decision about where we are going. Or if you have already committed to becoming a disciple of Jesus, I will remind you where you have committed to go so that we will remain focused in our efforts to arrive at our intended destination. In life, we have to decide where we want to go and how we are going to get there. We need to decide what is and is not worth living for and dying for. The most important decision that anyone makes in this life is how to respond to the love of God in Christ Jesus. The ultimate question that confronts each of us when we consider Jesus Christ and the claims of Christianity is, "Where Are You Going?" If Jesus were to ask you that question directly, how would you answer it?

Ultimately, Jesus asks each of his followers where they are going. In fact, he asks them to commit to being obedient to his commands. He asks them to live the kind of life that he calls all of his followers to live. In Matthew 16:24-28, Jesus says to his disciples:

> Whoever wants to be my disciple must deny themselves and take up their cross and follow me. For whoever wants to save their life will lose it, but whoever loses their life for me will find it. What good will it be for you to gain the whole world, yet forfeit your

soul? Or what can you give in exchange for your soul? For the Son of Man is going to come in his Father's glory with his angels, and then he will reward everyone according to what they have done.

It sure sounds like this is coming from someone who expects obedience from those who would follow him.

Yet not everyone has agreed that Christians ought to be people who actually live like Jesus told us to live and do the things that Jesus told us to do. As people have looked at the details of Wesleyan discipleship, or more generally the details of the teachings of Jesus in the New Testament, they typically react in one of three different ways. In this final chapter, I will examine each of these responses. I hope to demonstrate convincingly that the last response is the best, and the one that Jesus wants each of us to make. The question for Christians isn't whether we will respond to the gospel, but how we will respond to the gospel.

Before we talk about each of the specific responses, please understand that my point is not that Wesleyan discipleship is the only faithful way to be a Christian. There were countless men and women who lived for Jesus hundreds of years before Wesley was even born. Wesley was conscious that he was building on the foundations of those who had gone before him. There have certainly been many men and women after Wesley who creatively and faithfully lived for God and were not Wesleyan. My point is not that this is the only way, but that the Methodist way is a fruitful method for becoming a disciple of Jesus Christ. We are, after all, becoming followers of Jesus, not John Wesley!

What are the three reactions people typically have when the full expectations of Christian discipleship confront them? The first reaction is dismissive. Someone who has this reaction will say something like, "Hey, you need to lighten up! Why are you being so serious? Relax." This reaction subtly (or sometimes not so subtly) ridicules a serious commitment to discipleship as too uptight and obsessive about the things that people need to do in order to be a Christian. This approach also suggests that Wesley's standard is not only unreasonable, but also it is unnecessarily high.

People react dismissively for a variety of reasons. Some folks are reacting based on a hyper understanding of justification by faith. The argument is that it is not necessary for us to do anything except believe. As a result, faithfulness and obedience become irrelevant as long as you have faith. If the most important thing is to have the right beliefs, actions can become irrelevant. According to this line of thinking, it miraculously becomes possible to be a Christian without ever living like one. One can see why it would require a substantial leap of faith to believe that God delights in followers who say they believe in God but live as if they are their own gods.

Another reason people react dismissively is that they may be cultural Christians. Some people who grow up in the church mistakenly get the idea that being a Christian is not about a new way of life, but is part of the packaged deal that comes with being a "good American." These folks may even get angry if you criticize something related to American patriotism. Interestingly, they may be less likely to get similarly angry if you criticize something to do with Christian practice. There is an unspoken understanding that we don't really have to take the teachings of scripture seriously, we just have to give them a nod and a wink. We have to pretend as if we believe in the authority of scripture even though we never actually allow it to be an authority for how we live our own lives.

No matter why people undermine the importance of following Jesus, the important question to ask in light of such a reaction is: Is Wesley's understanding of discipleship a faithful articulation of what we find in the Christian scriptures? My argument throughout the course of this book suggests that it is.

The second reaction that people often have to the requirements of Christian discipleship is a detached appreciation or admiration. Christians who have this reaction and hear Wesley's story often react with surprise, and they typically emphasize what an amazing person he must have been. The tendency is to elevate him to such a lofty status that "normal" people can't be expected to live like that. I often feel uncomfortable when we talk about people like John Wesley or Mother Teresa because we admire them from afar in a way that distances and protects us from living the kinds of lives that they lived. The reality is that putting someone up on a pedestal keeps us from being open to the possibility in our own lives of living fully for God.

It is interesting that this reaction is similar to the reaction that many people have when they read the Sermon on the Mount. We read Jesus' command to be perfect as God is perfect, and we say, "Impossible!" Alternatively, we read Jesus' command to love our enemies, and we say, "That would never work!" People have often come up with very persuasive, even convincing, reasons why we should dismiss Jesus' teaching. It is interesting how creative we can be in coming up with reasons for why we should not follow the obvious teachings of scripture. Yet we are not willing to be nearly so creative when it comes to finding ways to actually live the way that Jesus teaches us to live. This seems to be an inadequate response. Instead of revealing a humble admission of our own imperfection, it more clearly reveals an unwillingness to obey Jesus' teachings. Again, the argument of this book suggests that we can do better and that God wants more for us.

Where I Hope You Will Go

Finally, I suggest the most fruitful response, that of awakening and repentance. When we recognize the expectations that come with the Christian life, we recognize that there is so much more to being a Christian than we have often suspected. We have too frequently settled for a weak God only occasionally and unpredictably involved in our lives. In reality, we worship a God who wants to lead us home. We need to reawaken to the power and vitality of our spiritual heritage. We need to repent of our apathy and our spiritual complacency. We ought to lament our frequent failure to be good stewards of the powerful tradition that has been entrusted to us and then work to reclaim—in Wesley's words—both the "form and power of godliness."

This response would recognize that there is value and power in what has happened before us. It would also realize the extent to which we have wandered away from deeply committed discipleship and settled for far less over the years. Ultimately, the ideal response would be to turn away from nominal Christianity, humble ourselves, and return to the method behind Methodism. After repenting, we would pray as one people that God would bless what God has blessed before once again!

We need to turn away from having faith in what we can do by our own powers and place our faith in what God is able to accomplish through us by God's power. God calls each of us to some specific task. God wants to use every one of us. We may be tempted to put people like John Wesley or Mother Teresa up on a pedestal and say, "I can never be like that." But we have so many examples of people who are "normal" and do amazing things for God through simple acts of faith. Recently, I heard a woman talk about the year that she spent in Africa. She lived for an entire year in the midst of a people and culture that were radically different from her own. She took an amazing risk not because she is so different from us, but because she heard God's voice calling her, and she said, "Yes." The difference between the heroes of the faith and us may be a difference in willingness to be out of control. Each of us can be a part of God's work in this world if we choose to follow wherever God leads us.

There are examples of "normal" people living faithfully in each of our churches and communities. We will find them if we will listen carefully to the stories they tell about how God is at work in their lives. But you should be careful if you do listen because you just might find that the one who is being called to step out in faith is you. Do you know where you are going? Are you headed in God's direction or somewhere else? Go to God and you will find that you are headed toward home. Finding our home with God is, after all, what the Wesleyan blueprint for discipleship is all about.

1. If Jesus were to ask you, "Where are you going?" how would you respond?

2. How does the direction that your life is heading affirm or contradict what you say is most important to you?

3. How does the way that you spend your time and your money reveal your commitment to following Christ?

4. What steps are you going to take to move toward becoming a deeply committed disciple of Jesus Christ as a result of reading this book?

Endnotes

1. <http://rinkworks.com/said/yogiberra.shtml>, accessed May 13, 2008.

Appendix A
The General Rules

This appendix includes the entire essay in which John and
Charles Wesley laid out the Methodist blueprint for discipleship.
The essay is called "The Nature, Design, and
General Rules of the United Societies," often referred
to simply as "The General Rules."

The Nature, Design, and General Rules of the United Societies in London, Bristol, Kingswood, and Newcastle upon Tyne (1743)[1]

1. In the latter end of the year 1739 eight or ten persons came to me in London who appeared to be deeply convinced of sin, and earnestly groaning for redemption. They desired (as did two or three more the next day) that I would spend some time with them in prayer, and advise them how to flee from the wrath to come, which they saw continually hanging over their heads. That we might have more time for this great work I appointed a day when they might all come together, which

from thenceforward they did every week, namely, on Thursday, in the evening. To these, and as many more as desired to join with them (for their number increased daily), I gave those advices from time to time which I judged most needful for them; and we always concluded our meeting with prayer suited to their several necessities.

2. This was the rise of the United Society, first at London, and then in other places. Such a Society is no other than 'a company of men "having the form, and seeking the power of godliness", united in order to pray together, to receive the word of exhortation, and to watch over one another in love, that they may help each other to work out their salvation'.

3. That it may the more easily be discerned whether they are indeed working out their own salvation, each Society is divided into smaller companies, called Classes, according to their respective places of abode. There are about twelve persons in every class, one of whom is styled *the Leader*. It is his business:

(1). To see each person in his class once a week at the least; in order
To receive what they are willing to give toward the relief of the poor;
To inquire how their souls prosper;
To advise, reprove, comfort, or exhort, as occasion may require.

(2). To meet the Minister and the stewards of the Society once a week, in order:
To pay in to the stewards what they have received of their several classes in the week proceeding;
To show their account of what each person has contributed; and
To inform the Minister of any that are sick, or of any that walk disorderly and will not be reproved.

4. There is only one condition previously required in those who desire admission into these societies, 'a desire to flee from the wrath to come, to be saved from their sins'. But wherever this is really fixed in the soul it will be shown by its fruits. It is therefore expected of all who continue therein that they should continue to evidence their desire of salvation,

First, By doing no harm, by avoiding all evil in every kind—especially that which is most generally practised. Such is:

> The taking the name of God in vain.
>
> The profaning the day of the Lord, either by doing ordinary work thereon, or by buying or selling.
>
> Drunkenness, *buying or selling spirituous liquors*; or *drinking them* (unless in cases of extreme necessity).
>
> *Fighting*, quarrelling, brawling; brother 'going to law' with brother; returning evil for evil, or railing for railing; the 'using many words' in buying or selling.
>
> The *buying or selling uncustomed goods.*
>
> The *giving or taking things on usury.*
>
> *Uncharitable* or *unprofitable* conversation, especially *speaking evil of ministers or those in authority.*
>
> Doing to others as we would not they should do unto us.
>
> Doing what we know is not for the glory of God, as,
>
> The 'putting on of gold or costly apparel', particularly *the wearing of calashes, high-heads, or enormous bonnets*;
>
> The *taking such diversions* as cannot be used in the name of the Lord Jesus,
>
> The *singing* those *songs*, or *reading* those *books*, which do not tend to the knowledge or love of God;
>
> Softness, and needless self-indulgence;
>
> Laying up treasures upon earth;
>
> Borrowing without a probability of paying: or taking up goods without a probability of paying for them.

5. It is expected of all who continue in these societies that they should continue to evidence their desire of salvation,

    Secondly, By doing good, by being in every kind merciful after their power, as they have opportunity doing good of every possible sort and as far as is possible to all men:

    > To their bodies, of the ability which God giveth, by giving food to the hungry, by clothing the naked, by visiting or helping them that are sick, or in prison.
    >
    > To their souls, by instructing, *reproving*, or exhorting all they have any intercourse with; trampling under foot that enthusiastic doctrine of devils, that 'we are not to do good unless *our heart be free to do it.*'
    >
    > By doing good especially to them that are of the household of faith, or groaning so to be; employing them preferably to others, buying one of another, helping each other in business—and that so much the more because the world will love its own, and them only.
    >
    > By all possible *diligence and frugality*, that the gospel be not blamed.
    >
    > By running with patience the race that is set before them; 'denying themselves, and taking up their cross daily'; submitting to bear the reproach of Christ, to be as the filth and offscouring of the world; and looking that men should 'say all manner of evil of them falsely, for their Lord's sake'.

6. It is expected of all who desire to continue in these societies that they should continue to evidence their desire of salvation,

    Thirdly, By attending upon all the ordinances of God. Such are:

    > The public worship of God;
    > The ministry of the Word, either read or expounded;
    > The Supper of the Lord;

Family and private prayer;

Searching the Scriptures; and

Fasting, or abstinence.

7. These are the General Rules of our societies; all which we are taught of God to observe, even in his written Word, the only rule, and the sufficient rule, both of our faith and practice. And all these we know his Spirit writes on every truly awakened heart. If there be any among us who observe them not, who habitually break any one of them, let it be made known unto them who watch over that soul, as they that must give account. We will admonish him of the error of his ways. We will bear with him for a season. But if then he repent not, he hath no more place among us. We have delivered our own souls.

John Wesley

Charles Wesley

May 1, 1743

Endnotes

1. *The Works of John Wesley,* Vol. 9. *The Methodist Societies: History, Nature, and Design,* ed. Rupert E. Davies (Nashville: Abingdon Press, 1989), 69-73. (Emphasis in original). Used by permission.

Appendix B
Guide for Small Groups

The goal of this guide is to introduce you to something similar to a Wesleyan class meeting as you work through this book. Ideally, this small-group experience will prompt members to want to continue meeting even after there is no longer a study to act as a reason for getting together. When we gather together to do nothing more than "watch over one another in love," we are in good company, as this is what the early Methodists were trying to do in the class meeting! The primary focus of the Methodist class meeting was the question "How is it with your soul?" Or, "How does your soul prosper?" The early Methodists asked one another this same question week after week. Through the class meeting, many Methodists came to have faith in Jesus Christ and experienced the new birth. Others grew in the faith that they already had and moved toward becoming deeply committed disciples of Jesus Christ. This guide is offered with the hope that taking the risk of revealing where we are in our relationship with God can be a powerful means of grace used by God to enable us to minister to one another and lead us closer to the God whom we worship as Father, Son, and Holy Spirit.

Once the group completes this study, it could continue meeting by omitting the section that deals with discussing the book and devoting the time together to discussing the questions "How is it with your soul?" or, "How does your soul prosper?" The group may also choose to substitute a short devotional or brief Bible study (about fifteen minutes) for the time together that had been focused on discussing the book. The group should keep in mind that the goal is not to convey what someone did over the past week but to discover where each person is in his or her relationship with God, and where God is calling him or her to grow in faith and love. The goal of the class meeting was not to gain more information; it was to be a vehicle for enabling people to actually become deeply committed disciples of Jesus Christ.

Gathering
Opening Prayer
Discussion of the Book

- What excited you or resonated with you about this week's reading?
- What challenged you or frustrated you about this week's chapter?
- What was confusing or did not make sense?
- How did this week's reading change your understanding of your faith and your relationship with God?
- Discuss and answer the questions at the end of the chapter.

The Class Meeting Questions
Each group member should have the opportunity to answer whichever form of the early-class-meeting question that the group is the most comfortable with:

- How is it with your soul?
- How does your soul prosper?

Sharing of Prayer Requests
Closing Prayer